The Fencers

Defection at the Olympics
A True Cold War Escape Story

ALSO BY GEZA TATRALLYAY

Arctic Meltdown (2011)

Twisted Reasons (2014)

For the Children (2015)

Cello's Tears (2015)

The Expo Affair (2016)

Twisted Traffick (2017)

Twisted Fates (2018)

Sighs and Murmurs (2018)

The Waffle and the Pancake (2018)

The Rainbow Vintner (2019)

Extinction (2019)

The Fencers

Defection at the Olympics
A True Cold War Escape Story

by

Geza Tatrallyay

Deux Voiliers Publishing

The Fencers is a memoir

First Edition 2019

Copyright © Geza Tatrallyay

All Rights Reserved

ISBN 978-1928049531

Published in Canada by

Deux Voiliers Publishing, Aylmer, Quebec.

www.deuxvoilierspublishing.com

Cover Design – Ian Thomas Shaw

Cover Photo – Geza Tatrallyay

For my friend, Paul, whose story this is

"The battles that count aren't the ones for gold medals. The struggles within yourself—the invisible, inevitable battles inside all of us—that's where it's at."

—Jesse Owens, four gold medals in track & field
Berlin, 1936 Summer Olympic Games

"He who is not courageous enough to take risks will accomplish nothing in life."

—Muhammad Ali, gold-medal boxer
Rome, 1960 Summer Olympic Games

FOREWORD

Geza Tatrallyay and I are both fencers. Geza and I are both fencers who immigrated to Canada from Eastern Europe seeking a better life. Geza and I are both immigrants who proudly represented our adoptive country on the world's biggest stage—the Olympic Games. While we competed over thirty years apart—Geza in 1976 and I in 2008—our lives took parallel paths that defined many aspects of our athletic careers, relationships and professional endeavours. It is a great pleasure to follow Geza along on a journey through life and around the world through his words—and to see pieces of my own journey in his. Although our athletic and professional paths never crossed, we will always remain fellow fencers, immigrants and Team Canada Olympians.

Geza's story is incredibly unique, yet the humility and simplicity with which he describes the most fascinating events make him relatable. *The Fencers* is an intimate experience with the book's author, one that gives us a chance to travel time and space to visit Expo '70 in Osaka, go on a road trip through Europe and walk into the opening ceremony of the Montreal 1976 Olympic Games. Yet *The Fencers* is more about the people Geza met than about the places he visited. Karl Marx once said: "Surround yourself with people who make you happy. People who make you laugh, who help you when you're in need. People who genuinely care. They are the ones worth keeping in your life. Everyone else is just passing through." Throughout his life, Geza surrounded himself with the most fascinating of characters—many passed through, but many stayed in Geza's life to this day.

One person who stayed in Geza's life is Paul. Paul Szabó is a Romanian-Hungarian fencer whom Geza helped defect to Canada during the Montreal 1976 Olympic Games. As Geza describes the adventure, it becomes evident that the experience is a test of emotional and physical strength for both Paul and Geza. The author downplays his heroic act, yet the words printed on paper punch holes of struggle and effort to remain strong for Paul—something that Geza never showed his friend throughout the process.

The Fencers is more than an Olympic journey—it is a fascinating account of Geza's life story—from immigration to Canada to life as a student-athlete and ultimately, to his Olympic experience and a transition to life after sport. Geza Tatrallyay is someone who lives every day of his life like it is his last. It is an absolute pleasure to experience this life well-lived through *The Fencers*.

Olya Ovtchinnikova
Team Canada Olympian, Beijing 2008

PREFACE

This is the third volume in my trilogy of Cold War Escape stories—all books about true events I was involved in when I was young—tales of daring, bravado, friendship and love. These stories are not unique: they are the narratives of immigrants like me, the shared experiences of many people who seek to leave their homeland behind in search of a better life, a brighter future for themselves and their loved ones.

The Fencers is also a sports memoir. It tells the story of how, as an eleven-year-old, I took up and pursued the sport of fencing, the characters I met and the friends I made through it, and the many interesting experiences the sport gave me over the years. But most of all, this is the account of a budding friendship between Paul Szabó, a Romanian-Hungarian fencer, and me, culminating in his impassioned approach to me to help him stay in Canada during the 1976 Montreal Olympics. It is the tale of his courageous and lonely defection, at the young age of twenty-one, and also of his love for a young woman whom he ended up marrying, and finally, of her untimely death and the tragic loss this was for Paul.

The story takes place at the height of the Cold War. In then communist Romania, the country Paul represented in the 1976 Olympics, Nicolae Ceaușescu was President. After a brief, early period of liberal rule, by then this tyrant had imposed strict Stalinist repression and terror. Mismanagement, rampant corruption, mass surveillance, brutality and human rights abuses characterized his régime. He and his secret police, the cruel Securitate, particularly singled out the large, almost two million in number, Hungarian minority living mostly in the former principality of Transylvania with their purges, oppression and restrictions of freedom.

In contrast, society in the West had taken a liberal turn at the end of the sixties and this was still evident throughout the mid-seventies, although with the 1973 oil crisis, a more conservative trend had set in. Nevertheless, the young continued to rebel against the excesses of capitalism and experiment with different lifestyles, both on and off campuses. Sexual freedom and drug use were still in vogue among twenty-somethings. Canada, under the leadership of Prime Minister Pierre Elliott Trudeau, stood out as a bastion of freedom, taking in refugees from all over the world, including American draft dodgers who did not want to serve in the Vietnam war, as well as boatloads of Vietnamese, Cambodian and Laotian refugees fleeing the ravages of war in South East Asia among countless others.

For Canada, the Games of the XXIst Olympiad, the first to be held in the country, were a particularly important event to showcase itself as a bicultural, indeed multicultural, success story. Following nine years after Expo '67, the world's fair also hosted by Montreal, still Canada's largest city at the time, Mayor Jean Drapeau and Prime Minister Trudeau saw the Olympics as an opportunity to build on the world-class recognition the metropolis and the country had attained. No expense was spared on the facilities and on preparations for these Games.

It was against this backdrop that the story of *The Fencers* unfolds.

For the rest, you will have to read the book.

I have enjoyed writing this and the other two memoirs in the Cold War Escape series: *For the Children*, the story of my own family's escape from Communist Hungary in 1956 during the Revolution and our subsequent immigration to Canada, and *The Expo Affair*, which tells about three Czechoslovak girls working in their country's Pavilion at Expo '70 in Osaka, Japan, who approached me, a host in the Ontario Pavilion at the time, to help them defect to Canada. But in writing this memoir, I have also had the great pleasure of rekindling my friendship with Paul Szabó, without whom this book would not have been possible.

I hope you enjoy reading it as much as I have delighted in writing it.

ACKNOWLEDGEMENTS

I am grateful to Ian Shaw for agreeing to publish this memoir and for his continued support of my work. Also, for taking the time to read *The Fencers*, for his editing and for his recommendations. Many thanks, too, to David Menear, a fellow Deux Voiliers author, for his methodical editing. To Olya Ovtchinnikova, a fellow Canadian Olympic fencer (2008) and the Program Manager for the Canadian Olympic Committee for writing a Foreword for the book and for all the support she is giving me.

My deepest gratitude goes to Paul Szabó for his courage in making this story happen, for letting me write about it and for his many helpful suggestions. But most of all, for being a friend.

And my thanks, too, to all the other participants in this wonderful tale.

Chapter 1

Fencing. The notice on the bulletin board said fencing classes would start on Tuesday after school at four o'clock. Come and learn what real swordsmanship is all about. With Maître Julius Alpár, the famous Hungarian Olympic fencing coach.

It was September 1960 and I had just begun my first year at U.T.S., the University of Toronto Schools, a top academic school in Toronto associated with the University, which used it to train teachers. My family was still relatively new to Canada; we had escaped from Hungary and immigrated just four years earlier. My father's brother and sister had both come to this land of the future after the Second World War, and my parents had been desperate to follow and leave Stalinist oppression in Hungary to give their children a decent life in a free country. So during the chaos of the Revolution in 1956, we tried to leave three times, and were caught twice, succeeding to get to Austria on the third attempt after a harrowing escape. I wrote down the story of our escape much later so that my family would have it, and it is now a book, *For the Children*.

Canada was a very welcoming country then, as it still is, and first we went to live in a small town, Peterborough, Ontario, where my uncle Gabriel worked and lived with his new Canadian family. We moved to Toronto two years later, at the urging of Béla Szandtner, one of my father's friends from Hungary who had come to Canada soon after the end of the war, to join him in the import business he had started. I first attended St. Anselm's, a Catholic school in Leaside, where we lived close to my father's place of work. But when I was ready to go into Grade 7, which is when U.T.S. started, my parents wanted me to sit for the entrance exams. It was this school that the sons of my father's partner were attending, and it was they who strongly recommended it to us as the best school in Toronto. And my parents, as new Canadians, listened to the advice of their friends who had been in the new country for a lot longer. So they were very pleased that I managed to get into this first-class school. As was I, because by this time, I was somewhat bored with the parochial Catholic teaching at St. Anselm's and keen to try new things.

I was rather intrigued and surprised though, to learn that my new school would offer fencing along with all the more Canadian sports, such as hockey and football, and even more so, that the coach was Hungarian.

I brought the subject up over dinner.

"Alpár Gyula!" my father exclaimed, standing up. He, too, was very surprised. "Amazing! Alpár was Professor of Physical Education and Fencing at the Hungarian Military Academy before the war. The famous Ludovika."

"Where Loránt went?" my mother asked. Loránt was my father's sister's husband, and after the war, they had ended up first in Algiers and then in Montreal, coming to Canada in the footsteps of Gabriel, my uncle.

"Yes. I am sure he knew Alpár. But more importantly, Alpár trained many Hungarian Olympic medal winners. Come to think of it, Géza, he must have known your grandfather from the 1936 Olympic Games in Berlin. Alpár coached the Hungarian saber team in Berlin, where, as you know, Apa was the team doctor. Yes, I remember now, he thought very highly of him."

"You should definitely sign up for the sport, Géza," my mother said. "Especially if you can have such an excellent teacher. And, of course, you should mention your grandfather ..."

"Besides, fencing is Hungary's national sport," my father added. "And I did it in my youth. Foil. It was a lot of fun, I can tell you."

I DID SHOW UP in the gym after classes the following Tuesday. Yes, partly because after the discussion around the dinner table I was curious to see who this famous 'Olympic' coach was, but more so because fencing had a romantic aura associated with it. Still not in my teens at the time, I had visions of emulating Ferenc Rákoczi, the swashbuckling Prince of Transylvania who became a Hungarian hero by leading a rebellion against the Austrians in the early part of the eighteenth century. Or dreams of teaming up—much as d'Artagnan did—with the Three Musketeers, with Athos, Porthos and Aramis. I had read the Dumas novel twice, first in Hungarian and then in English. Or simply of rescuing fair damsels from dragons.

And my father's mention of Apa and the Olympics had brought back memories of my maternal grandfather and namesake, who had passed away that very summer. Tragically, just before finally getting the exit permit from the Communist government in Hungary that would have allowed him and my grandmother to visit us in Canada for the first time since we escaped in 1956 during the Revolution. I never saw my grandfather again after we left Hungary when I was seven years old.

Baitz Géza had been the official doctor of the Hungarian team during the 1936 Berlin Olympics. And, as a young child, I had fond memories of sitting on his lap as we flipped through a large, fading red canvas-bound book on the Berlin Games, with the Olympic rings engraved in gold on the cover. We would be looking for the two or three photos in which my grandfather appeared, debonair with his close-trimmed moustache, dressed in a white linen suit, posing with different sets of athletes.

But my favorite pictures in the book were those action shots of Jesse Owens, the great African-American track and field star who so upset Adolf Hitler by winning four gold medals. And of course, those of the Hungarian fencers, Kabos Endre and Elek Ilona winning gold in individual saber and women's foil fencing along with the entire saber team. In fact, Kabos' two golds must have irked Hitler too, since he was also Jewish.

These phenomenal stars were my idols, and here was my opportunity to try to emulate them in my own small way. Although the Olympics were another thing altogether. Let alone gold medals.

THE FIRST LESSON did not go well. Alpár was an excellent coach, and started out with the basics. But after all the build-up by my parents, I was disappointed to find that training for the sport was fundamentally boring and a lot of hard work. For one, all the moves were so unnatural and difficult. A lot of moving backward and forward with knees bent, holding the arms in rather uncomfortable, strained positions. I was completely exhausted after that first experience; all my muscles ached and I considered quitting. But the Maître encouraged me, and his presence kept reminding me of my childhood heroes, especially the Olympic ones. Also, I found it rather agreeable—although somewhat weird—to have someone speak Hungarian to me at the school. So I stuck with it from one training session to the next.

For the fourth lesson, Maître Alpár brought another man with him. Balding and distinguished looking, this gentleman was also suited up with the heavy fencing vest and above-the-elbow glove typically worn by fencing masters.

What, two professional coaches for the seven or eight beginners who regularly showed up Tuesday and Thursday afternoons at this high school? And Olympians, at that! Wasn't that overkill? I asked myself.

But then Coach Alpár introduced the newcomer. "This is your new coach, Maître Imre Hennyey. Maître Hennyey is taking over from me as the trainer for the University of Toronto team and has agreed to teach at your school as well. He is an excellent fencer and coach, and was on the Hungarian Olympic team in 1948 and 1952, as an epéeist. You will do very well with him. As for me, I have been invited to teach at the University of California in Berkeley.

5

Maître Hennyey is taking over from me starting today."
Coach Alpár saluted with his foil and signaled to the new
fencing master to lead us in the communal warm-up
exercises.

That evening, I recounted this change in my fencing
fortunes to my parents.

"Well, I have heard of Hennyey Imre," my father said.
"Yes, he too, was an Olympian and a coach with a strong
reputation. But he is no replacement for Alpár. Alpár was
unique, even in Hungary. Shame. But no matter. Stick with
it, son."

IN MY OPINION, albeit, I admit, that of a total neophyte, Imre
Hennyey was every bit as good a coach as Julius Alpár,
maybe even better. Perhaps not as famous as his
countryman in the old snobby Hungarian circles, but I
found him more inspiring and engaged with us, and
technically very competent. For the next seven years, until I
graduated from grade thirteen at U.T.S. in 1967, I worked
with Maître Hennyey. Initially, I took just the twelve or so
lessons a year offered at the high school and only at foil, the
so-called training weapon. But after the first two years,
Maître Hennyey decided I was getting mature enough to
work with him over at the University of Toronto. So I would
go over to Hart House where the university team's fencing
salle was located whenever I could, and got extra lessons
from him. And Maître Hennyey switched me to epée, a
weapon much more suited to me, I found, and also probably
to my teacher, since that was the discipline he had fenced in
the Olympic Games. Occasionally, he even had one of the

university's epéeists fence against me, which, of course, for a mere high school boy, was a real thrill and honour.

Epée is the derivative of the rapier, the original dueling weapon. It is based on the concept of first blood, so there are no right-of-way rules as in foil and saber. Whoever lands the touch first, scores. There is also the concept of a double touch, where both fencers are awarded a point if they score within milliseconds of each other. Moreover, in epée, the whole body is the target, with hits to the wrist and the toe being classic ways to score since those are the closest parts of the opponent's body. It is also heavier than the other two weapons, and the point is calibrated so that the touch registers electronically only if it lands with a force of at least seven hundred and fifty grams. I often wondered how they calculated that this much force is required to draw blood; the experiments must have been gruesome and painful. In epée fencing, it also helps to be tall and lanky, which suited me perfectly.

Already with the foil, I had started to do well in some external junior meets, but with Maître Hennyey's solid coaching, I also began to win a few epée competitions, again mostly around Ontario.

Chapter 2

During my last year at U.T.S., the time came to apply to universities. I focused initially on Canadian schools, and I was keenest on the University of British Columbia in Vancouver, since I had heard that that was a fun city and a good place to study. Deep down, too, I was aching to put some distance between myself and the parental home. For no particular reason, since I loved my parents, other than perhaps a thirst for adventure and independence. McGill in Montreal was my second choice. Brock McMurray, the Headmaster at U.T.S. talked me into applying to Princeton, since several students from the school had gone there in years past. For both McGill and Princeton, one had to write the Scholastic Aptitude Tests, and at that time, the SAT administrators would send your scores to three schools for free. So, forever the bargain hunter, I needed to find a fourth university to apply to. Just the day before the tests, I had seen an article in Time magazine about Harvard beating Yale at a rowing regatta, so I decided on a whim to put Harvard down on the SAT form. I knew that it was a top university, and my chances of getting in were next to zero, nevertheless, I went through the motions of following up with an application.

Well, Harvard was the university that responded first and they offered me a great scholarship and lots of other financial assistance, which made it ultimately possible for an immigrant kid like me to go there. I was quite flattered, and wanted to respond positively right away. When I told the Headmaster though, he suggested I wait. Secretly, I think Brock McMurray wished he had gone to Princeton himself and that was his university of choice for his students. Princeton did come through with an acceptance but was a bit lighter on the financial assistance. A little later, McGill too, sent its acceptance. The only school I did not get into was the University of British Columbia, which, I learned later, had strict quotas for accepting out-of-province students. But by then, my heart was set on Harvard anyway.

No doubt, being a budding success at my sport must have played at least a small role in helping me get into Harvard. Although I don't think the fencing coach there could have paid much attention to the fact that on my application, I claimed to be engaged in the sport and had won a few unknown parochial competitions in Canada. He was much more focused on a crop of excellent freshmen fencers coming from the New York area. Tom Keller was a beautiful foil fencer and had won many junior competitions around New York, the hub of the sport in North America at the time. Larry Cetrulo came from a family of topnotch Italian-American sabreurs. Mark Irvings was an up and coming epée fencer with a solid record acquired at various New York and New Jersey high school competitions. So he had all three weapons covered. I must have been his wild card, and Coach Marion probably only took a chance on me because of my Hungarian background. As I learned later, he was Eastern European himself, from Yugoslavia, or more specifically, Slovenia.

Fencing with these guys on the freshmen team at Harvard was great fun. Mark and I often sparred in epée, which is what I now concentrated on. There was not a lot to separate us, except that his style was much more polished and classical than mine. We became great friends. I also convinced a couple of friends in my freshmen dorm—Grays East—George Spyrou and Pat Pankhurst, to come out for the team. George ended up being the hero of our match against Cornell, winning his last foil bout five to four, which gave us the victory fourteen wins to thirteen losses. When he got the winning touch in the tight match, we ran out on the piste and tossed him in the air several times amid loud cheers.

To these away contests at other Ivy and non-Ivy Universities, we shared a bus with the Varsity team; Coach Edo Marion, a former officer in the Yugoslav army, would sit up at the very front while there would be a lot of drinking and dope smoking happening in the back, especially on the return trips late at night. Although he never commented on these more nefarious, post-competition activities, we were quite positive that he knew exactly what was going on in the back of the bus.

With the daily training sessions under Coach Edo and frequent exposure to competition, my fencing, or should I say rather my results, steadily improved. I think, though, Coach Edo despaired when he watched my bouts, because I was so eager to score that I often lost my balance and fell over, ending up with torn stockings and bloody knees from scraping them on the fine copper mesh piste on which the fencing matches took place. Falling, though, seemed to me to be not a bad tactic, because it allowed me to roll away from the point of my opponent, plus I had a very good chance of hitting him as I quickly jabbed upwards before the referee called a halt. My fellow team members would often laugh and roll their eyes, but as long as I managed to eke out a win, they, and the Coach, were happy. Notwithstanding my technical faults, I had good reflexes, and I was in good condition.

Thus, by the end of my sophomore year, I had improved so much that I achieved All-Ivy honors. But just: I had to win my last bout against Yale, a cliff-hanger that went to four to four before I got the last touch. Coach Edo selected me to go the Nationals, the NCAA Championships in Raleigh, North Carolina that year, where I did not perform well, coming only sixteenth out of forty-five starters. Both Larry and Tom fenced exceptionally well, so as a team we were All-American and second overall. Larry has never forgiven me for not doing better because that cost us winning the NCAA team trophy for Harvard.

However, this one time I thought I could honestly push the blame onto someone else: Coach Marion. He had forgotten to reserve a room for us at the hotel near the venue, and eventually, after much negotiation at the front desk, it came down to Tom, Larry and me sharing a room with only two single beds. Of course, it was Tom and Larry who got the beds, since they truly had a good chance at a good result, while I, the 'wild card', slept on the floor. But 'slept' is perhaps overstating it: we thought that since we

11

didn't have proper accommodation, it would be unfair for the other teams to get a good night's sleep. So, as a prank, we called their rooms one by one and Tom played his harmonica over the line while Larry and I sang Italian and Hungarian ballads in the background.

MY SOPHOMORE FENCING SEASON came to an end with the Nationals, and somewhat reluctantly, I said goodbye to Coach Marion and the team. For, by this time, I had informed them that I would be taking a year's leave of absence from Harvard to work in the Ontario Pavilion at Expo '70, the world's fair being held in Osaka, Japan that year. I had applied for this job on a lark, and was happily surprised when they accepted me.

It would be a timely break in my academic career, since I was quite lost and did not really know what I wanted to study. I had first tried my hand at majoring in Geology, attracted by the planned field trip during the spring break to the Bahamas to study coral reefs, but I was sorely disillusioned once this excursion was canceled. I switched to Government, but found it boring and wanted to drop it.

But change to what?

I needed some time off to think and figure things out for myself.

Plus, working at Expo '70 could be a fun adventure in an exotic, faraway country. Nevertheless, the Coach urged me to keep up the fencing if I could during the summer in Canada and then the rest of the year in the Far East, although he admonished me to stay away from kendo, "because that would only make your already flailing moves even wilder" as he put it.

I had become quite fond of Coach Marion, and, I think, he of me. Perhaps was it because I was the only Central European on his team? I don't really know, but he sent me a delightful and rather touching note before I finally set out from Toronto for Japan in February 1970 with the other Ontario hosts and hostesses. The letter was peppered with what must have been word for word translations of Slovenian expressions and countless grammatical and spelling mistakes. I reproduce some of his message here:

"Of course you are a perfect angel with burned down wings and growing horns. Nevertheless, Devils like you are in demand. All kiddings apart, you are really a very fine young man. I will be happy and glad if there will be anything I will pass or contribute to your already fine personality.

We as team most certainly miss you very much and we are hardly waiting for next fall for your return with an effect as the Sunshine after a long Winter.

We all wish you a very happy and joyfull staying in Japan. I do hope you will not in this time switch your taste for Spirits from slivovitz to sukiyaki ..."

> *Yours*
> *Coach*

P.S. We will struggle to keep our placement of last year in the Ivy. The sophomores are very weak and practically no talent for fencing.

As a word of explanation: 'slivovitz', the Slavic version of the firewater made from plums everywhere in Eastern

13

Europe, was Coach Marion's choice of drink to sip or for a toast. 'Sukiyaki' though, as most people will know, is a Japanese beef dish, which, I surmised, the former Yugoslav army officer must have confused with 'sake', the rice wine *nihonjin* are famous for.

Chapter 3

After Expo '70, I wanted to travel back through Asia, thinking this might be a once in a lifetime opportunity, for which it was worth missing the first few days of school. So I wrote to the Dean at Harvard, and was pleasantly surprised when he wholeheartedly supported the idea, saying a trip like that would be better education than anything Harvard could provide.

So I traveled for almost a month, flying from Japan to Bangkok, then to Rangoon, now Yangon, in then Burma, now Myamar, then on to Dacca in what was still East Pakistan and now is Bangladesh, thence to Katmandu in Nepal, followed by Calcutta and Delhi in India, with a side trip to Agra to see the Taj Mahal, then on to Kabul in Afghanistan, and lastly, Teheran in Iran, where I also visited my Slovak girlfriend from Expo '70, Sasha, whose father was working for UNESCO in Esfahan. After this remarkable trip, visiting many countries that were essentially closed to tourists for many years, I flew back to Boston through Istanbul. Here, as I was boarding my Lufthansa flight, they took away my prized *kukri*, the curved knife used by the Gurkhas to fight against the British, that I had bought in Nepal, only to give it back when I finally arrived in the USA. I have kept it to this day as a memento of my visit.

Although this trip was a great adventure and a lot of fun, certainly the icing on the cake after Japan, I was now eager to return to Harvard. Not just to see my friends, but I must confess, after the rather hedonistic experience of traveling, playing and partying at Expo '70, I was thirsting for intellectual stimulation. I was also keen to get back to fencing and regular physical activity. The few training sessions at Kansei University I had attended with my beautiful Czechoslovak hostess friend, Zozana, were really not enough to prevent me from losing the edge. And wild dancing at the many parties and the random pick-up midnight volleyball games with other hosts and hostesses in Higasi Mati, the apartment complex near Osaka where the foreign staff were all housed, did not provide enough cardio exercise to keep me in good shape.

Back at Harvard, my roommates were enthusiastic to see me, as I was them. I moved into a five-bedroom suite in Adams House with George Spyrou, Don Gogel, Rob Cameron and Pat Pankhurst. They regaled me with their stories of the year I had missed: 1969-70 was the year of the Kent State shootings, when at Harvard and other campuses around the USA there were huge anti-Vietnam War demonstrations. Of course, Vietnam was a big issue for my American friends, and many of them were concerned about the draft and the lottery system. As a Canadian, I was lucky to be an exempt bystander to the trauma my American friends were living.

The concern with the draft and Vietnam brought back visions of Jeb, the private fighting with the US army in South East Asia who had come for R&R to Expo '70 and whom my roommate Malcolm McKechnie had taken pity on when he saw him drinking several beers all by himself at the Bierstube in the München Pavilion. Since Jeb had no place to sleep, Mal invited him to stay in the apartment we shared with another friend, Jeremy Smith, in Higasi Mati. For all I knew, poor Jeb was probably dead by now: seeing the fun and freedom in our lives, for a brief moment in Japan he had considered deserting, but was just too afraid to face the possible consequences.

What a contrast in fates, in what is important!

PAT AND GEORGE—the roommates I had enticed into coming out for the freshman team—were no longer fencing. Pankhurst had become a heavy user of drugs and some of us feared that he may have short-circuited some brain functions. He bought an old motorcycle that he moved into his bedroom, and spent several weeks, totally stoned night and day, disassembling it and then putting it back together again. He would rev the engine up in the middle of the night, eliciting angry yells from the rest of us.

George was … well, just George, a wonderful friend who was always fun to be with. Many girls must have thought that too, because he didn't have any trouble going from girlfriend to girlfriend during those Harvard years.

I, ON THE OTHER HAND, was hungry to get back to fencing. So soon after registering, already three weeks into the new term, the fencing salle in the Indoor Athletic Building was one of my first stops. Coach Marion and my friends on the team welcomed me enthusiastically, although Larry still could not help ribbing me about my poor performance at the Nationals in our sophomore year.

It did not take me long to polish my individual style, and I found that my reflexes, which had always been my main asset in the sport, had not really suffered from the lack of training and all the heavy partying at Expo '70.

However, because I had been away from regular athletic activity, I stupidly managed to injure myself playing for Adams House in the intramural soccer league. I tore ligaments in my knee and for the first few months back, I was hobbling around on crutches. While this brought me a lot of sympathy especially from the ladies, it did keep me away from fencing. But not being able to train every day also gave me more free time to develop my budding relationship with Laurence, a French girl at Adams House I had become quite keen on.

I was itching to get back on the piste, though, and I was very discouraged when the doctor at the Harvard Medical Center said that I would need a knee operation. This was not what I had wanted to hear, especially since it would entail a long recovery period, essentially keeping me away from my sport for the rest of that year. At the urging of my friends, I decided that I would consult another doctor, and this one, fortunately, said that with lots of the right exercises to strengthen the muscles around the joint, I might be able to avoid surgery. So that is what I did, and within a couple of months, I was back on the piste with the team.

Nevertheless, this junior year was not a strong one for me from a fencing standpoint. Coach Edo was frustrated with my lack of results and took Mark Irvings to the Nationals instead to round out the team with Larry Cetrulo and Tom Keller. I was disappointed, but glad when the team chose me as Captain for the following year.

SENIOR YEAR AT HARVARD, on the other hand, turned out to be a very good one. The summer before, with my Expo '70 experience, I had landed a job as a host at Ontario Place, the new exhibition and entertainment grounds in Toronto right down on the lakefront, and in the evenings when I was free, and not partying, I was able to train with yet another Hungarian-Canadian coach, Fred Wach.

Back at Harvard that fall, since my original roommates had graduated, I went into a triple in Adams House with Verdi di Sesa, a lacrosse player from a well-to-do Philadelphia Italian-American family, and one of my fencing buddies, Terry Valenzuela from Arizona. He and I were the backbone of the team that year, and Terry, a sabreur, followed me as Captain the next year, and as a Rhodes Scholar the year after.

I was in top form for fencing. Maybe it was because I led a balanced life: I had a great girlfriend, fun roommates and was finally stimulated by my studies in Human Ecology under the mentorship of Roger Revelle. I made All-Ivy again, leading Harvard to second place, its best ever performance up until then in the fencing Ivies. And, at the Nationals in Chicago, I placed fourth in the individual event to make All-American. This time, the Coach was indeed proud of me.

COACH EDO WAS a smart man and had excellent intuition. One day in early April, after the collegiate fencing season had more or less drawn to an end, he collared me after a bout.

"You Devil. I see you won again. Good." Coach Edo was not one for too many compliments. "Géza, you are Canadian, no? I see Olympic trials in your country start May twentieth. Why you not go and fence in them? Who knows, maybe you are good enough to make team in Canada. Only Eskimos there, they fence with harpoons against walruses. And often they lose. Your footwork already is like you fence on ice. So no problem. You fit in, maybe even win there."

I had trouble squelching my laughter, but I jumped at Coach Edo's suggestion; I hadn't even dared think that I might make the Canadian Olympic team, but maybe he was right ... why not give it a try? The Coach had put my dream right back in my mind, front and centre.

I went back to my room and registered just in time for the Canadian Nationals, which were also billed as the Olympic Trials. Then I arranged my affairs and flew up to Montreal at my own expense, and justified it, telling myself that, if nothing else, it would be an opportunity to see my grandmother who lived with my Aunt Klára just outside the city.

In the Nationals, I fenced better than I usually did, perhaps because I had nothing to lose and rose to the occasion. When the regular rounds were over, I was tied for first, but ended up losing the fence-off for the gold medal, five to four. John Andru, the head of the Canadian Fencing Association, told me afterward that had I won, they would have definitely taken me to the Olympics. After all, they could simply not not take the Canadian National Champion!

Andru also told me, however, that even though I had lost the national title and had not fenced in all the competitions in Canada where I might have earned the requisite points, there was still a chance that I could make the team. Apparently, George Váraljay, the recently escaped Hungarian who had beaten me in the fence-off for the Championship, did not yet have his Canadian papers and it was not a hundred percent sure that the Hungarians would release him to fence for Canada in the Olympics.

The head of the Canadian Fencing Association suggested that training hard during the coming summer would certainly help my case. So I asked my parents what they thought if I were to go to Hungary to fence there. Although, at first, they were against it—since I was very much of draft age and, as we had left without papers, the Communist authorities could just claim that I had never officially left Hungary, and there were, in fact, cases where young men who had gone back had been conscripted into the army— they eventually gave in. Through his connections, my father even arranged for me to train with the famous Hungarian National Pentathlon Team in Budapest. This was for the summer of 1972, after my graduation from Harvard.

So after the Commencement Ceremonies at the end of May, I said goodbye to my parents and friends, and off I went to Hungary. I stayed at my grandmother's on Kigyó utca in Budapest, right in the heart of downtown. I was the first one in the family to return since our escape sixteen years earlier, and she was delighted that she had me there for most of the summer. I found Hungary interesting and changed: under János Kádár, whom the Soviets had installed as head of state after the Revolution, starting in 1967, some freedoms and a limited form of capitalism had been introduced. This was what became known as "Goulash Communism".

In some ways, it was wonderful to be back in the city of my birth, but I did not feel completely at home. The imprint of Communism on the country was overwhelming, and I had perhaps become too westernized to be able to adjust completely.

Nevertheless, I trained hard with the pentathletes and my fencing improved a lot, even according to the exacting world-renowned fencing coach of the Hungarian Modern Pentathlon Team, Béla Bay. I was encouraged and thought I might have a good chance to go to the München Olympics.

A letter finally arrived from John Andru, and I tore it open excitedly. My jaw dropped in disappointment as I read it: the handwritten note said that they had decided not to take me to the 1972 Games. Váraljay's papers had come through and, in all fairness to the other Canadian fencers, I had not proved myself sufficiently by fencing in the specified Canadian competitions to amass the points needed.

Then and there, I vowed to myself that I would make the 1976 Olympic team.

Chapter 4

Fencing had become a big part of my life. I loved the physical activity, the thrill of the competition, the camaraderie. Especially now that I was starting to compete at an international level, there was also the travel and learning about other cultures, making friends with fencers from other countries. Moreover, the sport was playing a key role in shaping my fate: no doubt it had been partly responsible for getting me to Harvard, and my selection as All-Ivy and All-American and competing internationally in the sport must have played a role in helping me get the coveted Rhodes Scholarship from Ontario to study at Oxford University.

THE TWO YEARS at St. Catherine's College in Oxford were idyllic. I continued my studies in largely the same area I had created my major in at Harvard. I read Human Sciences, which had just been introduced as a discipline at Oxford University the year before and combined studies from genetics and animal behavior through to anthropology and sociology. There was very little class work, so I spent much of my time in Paris visiting Laurence, just coming back to college in time for the weekly tutorials. She had started to work as a fashion model in the City of Light, but in spite of my attempts to keep the relationship alive, we were slowly drifting apart, although I did not want to accept this.

Early after I settled into life at Oxford, I sought out the fencing team. I wanted to press ahead with my determination to make the Olympic team for the Montreal Games in 1976. I had done my research and the University had an excellent coach, another old Hungarian, Béla Imregi, who had been training fencers in Britain since after the Second World War, and was considered to be the number one fencing master in the United Kingdom at the time. Back in the old country, he had been a top pupil of the military fencing school, the Ludovika, the same one Julius Alpár had graduated from. In fact, he knew both Alpár and Hennyey and had probably also crossed paths with my grandfather, since in Berlin he was the coach of the 1936 Women's Foil gold medal winner, Elek Ilona.

I soon found that the freedom at Oxford allowed me the time to train in London as well, and to compete for Canada in meets around Europe. Coach Imregi also taught at the London Polytechnic Institute just above Oxford Circle, so I would go up once or twice a week to train with him. It also gave me the opportunity to fence with some prospective members of the British Olympic team who were being coached by him. As there were times when we trained well into the night, I often stayed over at a nearby friend's place, the daughter of the godfather of George, my roommate at Harvard, who was now over at Cambridge University and had introduced us.

The hard work started to pay off, because I got as far as the semi-finals in the British Nationals in June of 1973, my first year at Oxford. Unfortunately, these were held at the end of Trinity term and conflicted with my Human Sciences exams, so I was somewhat stressed out and not able to focus. But a bigger problem was that I managed to injure my knee again in the first round, and by the time the semi-finals came around, I was in considerable pain and my mobility was severely restricted.

By this time, John Andru saw my determination to fence internationally, and probably decided that it was cheaper to send me to events in Europe from the United Kingdom than to send others over from Canada. Fortunately, he and his colleagues at the Canadian Fencing Association included me in a select group of fencers who got some funding from the government to travel to competitions and to allay some of the training expenses in preparation for the 1976 Olympic Games, which for the first time Canada would be hosting. But more importantly, I was named to the national team for the World Championships in Göteborg, Sweden, to be held in July 1973.

I did not tell John Andru that I had been injured, and continued my training with Coach Imregi. I would sit on a chair and do drills with him to improve the fine hand movements and hand-eye control that is so key to fencing. Unfortunately, the legwork, also fundamentally very important to the sport, and which had always been my weak point, was totally neglected. Béla bácsi, 'Uncle Béla', as I called him in Hungarian, was there in Göteborg with the British team, and he would unselfishly spend a lot of his free time working with me.

It was exciting to represent my country in a major competition for the first time. I knew all the British fencers and had been up against most of the epéeists at one time or another in UK competitions. I also knew several members of the US team quite well: Brooke Makler, who used to fence for the University of Pennsylvania and had been my nemesis in the Ivies, and Scott Bozek was a Boston area fencer who was now one of the best epéeists in the USA. But it was here at the World Championships that I first really met the famous Hungarian team of Csaba Fenyvesi, Gyözö Kulcsár, Pál Schmitt, István Osztrics and Sándor Erdös. The five had won the team Olympic gold medal in München in 1972, and Fenyvesi had taken individual gold, with Kulcsár, the 1968 gold medallist, settling for bronze this time. Kulcsár had been on the 1964 and 1968 gold medal teams as well, while Fenyvesi and Schmitt had also won gold with the 1968 squad. So this was probably the most successful line-up of epée fencers of all time.

It was also in Göteborg that I came up against an excellent Romanian-Hungarian fencer, Paul Szabó, whose five to one victory over me was instrumental in knocking me out in the first round.

DURING MY SECOND YEAR at Oxford, I concentrated more on my studying and on fencing, and less on partying and women. In any case, my relationship with Laurence was foundering by this time. Also, I was actually enjoying the academic experience, two of my lecturers were Nobel Prize winners, and the readings in the philosophy of science, evolutionary biology, and social and biological anthropo-

26

logy were exhilarating. I was seriously attracted to an academic career.

The fencing, though, did not improve. I seemed to have plateaued, and although I competed in a number of international competitions throughout the year in Vienna, London, Bern, and Paris, I was not able to get past the second round in any of them. It was all very disappointing and stressful.

During spring break, between Hilary and Trinity terms, two Japanese friends from Oxford, Seiichi Kondo and Seiji Kojima, and I traveled to Greece through much of Southern Europe in Seiichi's car. We stopped in Budapest at my grandmother's long enough for me to fence in the Budapest International competition and for me to show Seiichi and Seiji around the city of my birth. This time, I did not make it past the first round. I was devastated and attributed the disaster to fatigue, both mental and physical.

Although I mentioned it to no one, I was seriously starting to worry about my fencing career. And my chances to make the 1976 Olympic team, although the Games were still some time in the future.

With my two Japanese friends, we continued our trip through Romania, which, in those years, was much more backward, poor and repressed than Hungary. The leadership under Nicolae Ceauşescu was two-faced: it presented a liberal, anti-Soviet approach to the West, but internally, it ruthlessly oppressed the population, especially the two million or so Hungarians, the largest minority group in Europe. Transylvania, where most of the Magyars lived, was traditionally a fiercely Hungarian province in the Austro-Hungarian Empire, and had been ceded to Romania under the terms of the Treaty of Trianon at the end of the First World War. Fundamentally, Ceauşescu wanted to wipe out all expressions of Hungarian culture, so teaching in Magyar was forbidden, Magyar names were forcibly changed, Hungarian monuments pulled down and history effaced.

The roads in the country were terrible and after one deathly scare, we simply did not drive at night because chauffeurs, especially truck drivers, just did not use lights. We were told that this was because they thought they were showing solidarity with the Communist workers' paradise by saving on electricity, which was clearly a rather stupid and preposterous explanation. I thought of looking up Paul Szabó, my Romanian fencer friend, but could not find his address.

In Bulgaria, approaching the Greek frontier, we picked up an East German hitchhiker. This poor young man tried to convince us to cross the border with him hiding in the trunk of Seiichi's car. A Lutheran minister's son, he had traveled all the way from near Dresden because he had heard that it was now easier to slip across the border from Bulgaria to Greece than anywhere else along the Iron Curtain. Much as I would have liked to take this fellow to his freedom, I did not want to spend the rest of my life in a Bulgarian jail, so I dissuaded my Japanese friends from letting him hide in the trunk. Sure enough, at the frontier, the border guards made a point of making a thorough search of the entire car.

I am sure my two Japanese friends were grateful to me later in life: both of them went on to stellar careers in the Gaimusyo, the Japanese Foreign Ministry, with Seiichi rising to become Deputy Secretary-General at the OECD and Ambassador to UNESCO and Seiji, Ambassador to Thailand. Spending several years in a Bulgarian prison would not have been a good start for either one.

WE CELEBRATED GREEK EASTER on Skiathos with my friend George Spyrou and his family: they entertained us with the typical celebrations, starting with a donkey ride up to the monastery at the top of the mountain, followed by a feast of the traditional organ soup of *maigeritsa* and red eggs, and then, as the *piéce de résistance*, an entire lamb roasted on a spit, accompanied by lots of fresh Greek salad with tomatoes, cucumbers, onions, olives and feta, and of course, many bottles of retsina, ouzo and tsipouro to drink. After several days of fun and frolic on the beaches of the island and in the bars of the village, we drove back through what was then Yugoslavia.

Even before we left England, I had signed up to fence in the Heidenheimer Pokal, the prestigious Class A international competition held every year in a cute little town in Germany. This was considered in the fencing world to be the toughest epée meet because all the top names in the sport would regularly attend. The Pokal was a competition where countries were not restricted to three or four entries per weapon, as in the Olympics or the World Championships, and many nations indeed brought eight or ten fencers to test them against world-class competition.

We arrived late on the evening before the day the event kicked off, tired and hungry. When I woke the next morning, I did not feel well, but once the fencing started and I saw some of my friends from the international circuit again, I began to enjoy it. But I was not in form and ended up going out in the second round.

Disappointed, I convinced my Japanese friends to drive to Paris, still that same day. They were all too happy, because there were no free rooms in the small town, and we would have had to sleep in the car.

AS MY SECOND YEAR at Oxford drew to a close, I did not feel I was quite ready to leave England and the idyllic student life, both of which I had come to really love and appreciate. So I asked the Warden of Rhodes House, Sir Edgar Williams, if I could spend a third year on the Rhodes Scholarship, and do so at the London School of Economics and Politics, to study for a Master of Science in Economics. The Rhodes had such a provision for a third year, which, with sufficient justification, did not have to be spent at Oxford, so I was delighted when the Warden graciously acquiesced.

One of the rationales for being in London rather than Oxford was because fencing was more competitive there, and of course, because I could spend more time working with Coach Imregi every day. Moreover, I had come to like the metropolis a lot, and it made it all potentially so much more fun that George and his brother, Alexander, were going to be living there. We found a flat together on Church Row up in Hampstead and lived a life of partying and luxury. George and Alexander were both working in the City, while I fenced and occasionally went to classes and put time in at the LSE library.

THIS YEAR, TOO, I continued to compete internationally, entering among others, the competition I had come to like the most, the Heidenheimer Pokal. I was determined to do well this second time around.

I easily made it out of the first round, and was quite pleased with the way I was fencing. I had won three bouts in the second round, and that would normally have been enough to advance to the next. Which would already be a phenomenal result for a Canadian fencer. To make the third round of a Class A international competition. And not just any meet, but the very tough Heidenheimer Pokal!

But I was not quite through yet. Two bouts in the pool remained. And both Sternowski, the Pole, and Pfigg, the local West German boy, could still end up with three victories, and in the case of a tie, touches for and against determined the ranking and ultimately who advanced to the next round. I had lost very badly against the top seed in the group, Sándor Erdös, the Hungarian, and had won two of my bouts, the ones against Sternowski and Pfigg, just by five to four, so my points for and against ratio was not all that good.

Sternowski was testing his point against the Italian Pezza's guard. Pezza was having an off day and I had managed to beat him five to three. There was a good chance that the Pole would defeat him too. But the last match would be Erdös, the Hungarian, against Pfigg, and Erdös had won a gold medal in the team epée event in München in 1972 and was still ranked in the top ten in the world, so that was a pretty sure outcome. Plus, all the Hungarians knew me, and we often went out drinking together after competitions. Erdös would surely not lose the bout to Pfigg, I told myself.

I was rooting for Pezza, but Sternowski got the first hit on Pezza's toe. The second hit was a beautiful feint attack to the body. The Pole was not bad. Christ, come on Pezza!

Not happy with the way this was going, I walked away toward the bench by the wall where I had left my gear. The Hungarian fencer was standing nearby, with his back toward me, and I was going to tell him that he had better win or I wouldn't buy him a beer that evening. But I realized he was talking to an older guy, and as I went closer, I saw this man give him some money, in fact, it was a big wad of Deutschmarks, which Erdös folded up in his hand and discreetly put in his fencing bag. It was only when this man went over to where Pfigg was warming up that I realized that he was the German fencer's coach. I understood immediately: the transaction was clearly to ensure that Erdös, who was already guaranteed a spot in the next round, dropped the bout against the local West German. For a tidy sum.

Sure enough, much to everybody's surprise, the Erdös-Pfigg bout went Pfigg's way. The Germans were ecstatic, and Pfigg got many pats on his back and congratulations from his compatriots. Erdös, Sternowski and Pfigg went up to the next round, while Pezza and I were eliminated.

I was livid and wanted to protest immediately. But what proof did I have of wrongdoing? The two culprits involved would no doubt vigorously deny the transaction. And I would only be seen as a sore loser. As the lone Canadian fencer and without a coach present, I had no one to turn to for help or counsel. Not even my Hungarian fencing friends, since it was one of them who had betrayed me. Disgusted, I picked up my fencing bag in a huff and went straight to the changing room.

I threw my bag in the corner and sat down on the bench. I buried my face in my hands. It was only when I looked up that I noticed two Romanian fencers, Popa and Dutu, sitting across from me, shoveling some spam-like food into their mouths from plastic containers. Just then, Paul Szabó, the tall, lanky Hungarian-Romanian fencer, whom I had seen and said hello to at other competitions, came into the dressing room. He had been fencing in another pool on the piste beside me.

"Szía," Paul greeted me with the Hungarian slang hello as soon as he saw me. He had pointedly come over to sit beside me as opposed to with his Romanian teammates. "How are you doing?" He must have seen the dejected look on my face. "Did you go through?"

"No. And you?"

"Okay. I made it to the next round."

"Congratulations."

Just then Iorgu, yelled something to Paul that I didn't understand in Romanian. He gave a curt answer back, before turning to me and asking, "Géza ... do you want to buy some blades? Iorgu wants to know. He will sell them cheap." It was well known in fencing circles that many Eastern European fencers sold state-issued equipment for hard currency. For pocket money, mainly to buy blue jeans and other Western fashionable clothing, as well as electronic gadgets.

"No thanks. Not now." I was not in the mood. Just very angry for having been cheated out of going into the next round. By a supposed friend, in fact. Huh.

Besides, I would not need any epée blades anymore if I quit fencing, which, at that very minute, I was seriously considering doing.

Paul relayed the message to his compatriot across the dressing room. An answer came back. I didn't give a damn. I just wished they would all go away.

But the next round would not start until after lunch, so they were not in a great hurry to leave me to my negative thoughts.

"Iorgu says he will sell them to you very cheap." And the Romanian fencer across the way took a batch of ten or so brand new epée blades out of his fencing bag and waved them at me. "He says he needs the money. He spent the five dollars our Federation gives each one of us last night and this morning, and would like to have some money for a warm meal tonight," Paul continued, a bit embarrassed. "Not a bad idea. I would, too, come to think of it," he added almost as an afterthought.

"What do you mean?" I asked, puzzled.

"We only eat the food we bring from home. So we can spend the little hard currency they give us on jeans. And other stuff to take back. The two over there . . . they are hungry after fencing and now they are eating the last of the food they brought from Romania . . . My stores are pretty well gone too."

I bought Iorgu's ten blades and did not even haggle. And I gave Paul the sandwich I had made for myself at breakfast in the hotel. Plus the apple I had taken for a snack.

I had been cheated out of a better placement in the competition, but these poor Romanian fencers were suffering a much greater injustice.

They were being cheated out of their dignity.

LSE EXAMS ROLLED around and I was totally unprepared. I had not attended all the classes, nor had the time, nor the inclination, to do all the reading for the four courses that I had to take. And, unlike all the other students enrolled in the Master's program, I did not have an undergraduate degree in Economics. But, although I was in somewhat of a pickle, I did not panic.

I went to the library and looked through the previous ten years of examinations. Just as I had thought, there were a core group of questions that appeared pretty well every year. With the help of some of my more brilliant economist friends, I wrote out answers to these questions and memorized them. Sure enough, my luck held and several of the very same questions appeared on the exams. I managed to do well enough to get my degree. I did not advertise, though, how.

It was at this point in my life that I had to make a serious choice. One option I had in front of me was to concentrate on making the Canadian Olympic team, for which I would have to go back to Canada to fence and do well in all the necessary competitions to collect enough points to have a chance of being named. I had learned my lesson in 1972. This Canadian option would also mean that I would be closer to my parents, and this had become rather important to me as my mother had been fighting breast cancer over the last several years.

The other option was to go back to Oxford and do a D. Phil, probably in Anthropology.

Or still a third choice, to Harvard, to work with my favorite professor and mentor there, Roger Revelle, on a Ph. D. in Environmental Studies.

They were all unique options, each with a lot going for it.

I chose the potentially most glamorous and easiest path.

Chapter 5

S o that decided it. I was going to Canada. Not to Oxford. Nor back to Harvard. I was abandoning my thoughts of pursuing an academic career. For a chance at the more immediate glory of making the Canadian Olympic team.

Still from England, I wrote to the Department of Environment in Ottawa about a job. I thought that was the most likely area I might get a job in, with my studies and background. I had found out that the Canadian Government had announced a program whereby it would give prospective Olympic athletes in its employ the necessary time off to train and compete. I needed a job to support myself, but I also wanted the time to fence. So this would be the perfect solution.

It was not until the late summer, most of which I spent working in the menial job of unpacking crates of Swedish stainless steel cutlery, crystal and porcelain in my father's firm, and well after I was back in Canada, that I finally received a letter from the federal government. But, as I tore the envelope open, I was suspicious because it had the Department of Finance as the return address on it. Not of

Environment, where I had sent my application. And quickly glancing through the letter, I saw that I was being asked to come to the capital for an interview with a Dr. E.P Neufeld, Director General for International Finance. Although somewhat surprised, because the little I knew about finance was what I had tangentially picked up in my Economics courses, I was intrigued by the 'international' sounding aspect of my prospective new employer. Little did they know how I had managed to get my Masters in Economics at LSE, I thought, if that was what they had focused on to offer me the interview.

Nevertheless, I went up to Ottawa and, to my great surprise, I got the job. It involved working with the Bretton Woods institutions, the World Bank and the International Monetary Fund, and Dr. Neufeld—who was also a graduate of the London School of Economics and Politics, and most recently, Professor of Economics at the University of Toronto—and John Coleman, the head of the International Finance Division under Neufeld, proved to be good bosses. I worked with a fun little group of colleagues, and I am thankful for the start this job gave me in the world of finance.

MORE IMPORTANTLY, my great friend Malcolm Mckechnie from Expo '70 was already in Ottawa working with the Department of External Affairs, living alone in a nice apartment with two big bedrooms on Charlotte Street in the Sandy Hill borough of the city, within walking distance of where I would be working. He was glad to have me move into the spare room and share the rent. And I was happy because we could continue the party atmosphere of Expo '70, albeit in a somewhat scaled back version.

THE OTHER GOOD THING about Ottawa was that one of the better fencing clubs in Canada was there: the Recreation Association, or RA, as it was commonly known. Certainly, from the standpoint of being in front of those who counted, this was the best club to belong to, for all the top brass of the Canadian Fencing Association, which after all, was headquartered in Ottawa, fenced or showed up here. The visibility was great, but I also managed to get good results that season, winning several local Canadian competitions, and placing reasonably well for a Canadian in some international ones John Andru and his colleagues selected for me to take part in.

Such as the Montreal International at the end of August and the beginning of September. Less than a year before the Olympics, this tournament was seen as the "practice" competition for the Olympics, and many of the world's best fencers had signed up to take part in it. The meet was held at the Winter Stadium of the University of Montreal, which is where all the fencing events at the Olympics were going to be held.

Unfortunately, I came down with a very high fever, starting already a few days before the competition. Two blisters on my right, or forward, fencing foot had become badly infected, and the doctor I went to gave me some antibiotics because he was concerned that it would develop into sepsis, or an infection of the bloodstream. He counseled me to rest and to stay away from stressful physical activity. But I simply could not withdraw from the competition because that would certainly have meant giving up my chances to make the Olympic team, as this was considered to be the best opportunity for the selectors to assess the form of the candidates and how they perform in an international event. So, at the meet, between each time I had to fence, since I had the chills, I would wrap my warm-up suit all over me and a towel around my head and I would lie down and stretch out on a bench to rest and try to recover for the next bout. I managed to come eighteenth, which for a Canadian, especially a very sick one, in a major international competition, was not too bad a result.

EARLY IN JANUARY of the Olympic year, seven of us who were in the core group from which the selectors would finally choose the teams for each of the weapons, were sent south to train in Cuba. The Cubans were aggressive fencers and had achieved respectable results in some major competitions. They had Russian or Hungarian coaches and were hard workers: for them, winning at the sport meant getting access to travel and luxury items. Working out with them was not a total success though, although it did let us gain more experience against international fencers. We found that, for some reason, even though it was just training, these Cuban fencers cheated whenever they could. Thinking about it, this must have been because they constantly had to show their coaches that they were on top, and they were probably competing more against each other for spots on the team than against us.

As a tragic aside, later that year, with a relatively uneventful Olympics in Montreal behind them, several of the fencers we had trained with in Cuba died in a horrific plane crash when Cubana Airlines Flight 455 blew up in the air after taking off from Seawell International Airport in Barbados. They were on their way to Jamaica to connect to a flight for home after winning all the gold medals in the Central American and Caribbean Championships. Many of the dead were still teenagers. There is strong evidence pointing to the cause of the crash being two bombs placed on the plane by anti-Castro Cuban exiles with links to the CIA.

But the trip to the Caribbean island did get us away from the Canadian winter, and to a vacation destination on the beach. As it happened, the fencing federation was not the only one in Canada that had the idea of a Cuban training camp: in fact, to our great surprise and delight, we discovered on the first evening at the bar that the Canadian women's volleyball team was staying at the very same resort. I got to know one of these girls, Julie (not her real name), a six-foot-two blonde, quite well. In fact, we spent several hours each evening, either out on the terrace of the room I shared with three fellow male fencers or down on the beach, becoming intimate with each other. Fortunately, neither of our coaches discovered this breach of curfew.

AFTER TROPICAL CUBA, I was glad to get back to my life in Ottawa. I enjoyed sharing the apartment with Mal and we had some good times. But I did not have much free time, since I worked at the Department of Finance during the day, and would come home only to change out of my suit and tie and collect my fencing bag, then race to go off to the club. Often, by the time I showered and socialized some with my fellow club members, I would not get back home until close to midnight. And on some weekends I would go off to compete somewhere in North America, and several times even to Europe.

I had no time for a serious girlfriend, but did have several fleeting affairs. Including with a number of lady fencers from the RA, and I learned the hard way that this was not necessarily a good idea. Whenever I showed up, I would feel the heat and tension go up a notch over on the women's side of the fencing salle. At such times, it felt good to hide behind a fencing mask and focus on beating my faceless opponents. Maybe I was just following in the footsteps of d'Artagnan, I consoled myself.

Mal and I decided that we would rent a cottage on the Gatineau River for the four summer months, so when the snows started to lift in April, we drove out there to look at the possibilities. Through one of his diplomatic contacts, we found a wonderful place right on the water with two little satellite cabins, presumably for guests. Most importantly, it was less than an hour away from downtown Ottawa where we both worked.

LATER IN APRIL, I flew down to New York for the Martini-Rossi tournament held every year at the New York Athletic Club. This was generally considered to be the most prestigious epée competition in North America, and indeed, since it was only four months before the Olympics, many top fencers from all over the world came to participate to hone their form. Including most of the American team, some of whom I knew from fencing on the collegiate circuit during my Harvard days.

I was in excellent shape for this meet and felt that I was fencing at my peak. I made it through to the third round, and was winning a crucial bout that would have put me into the semi-finals three zero against a first-class fencer, Nicola Granieri, who had won the 1971 World Cup and was Italian National Champion. I constantly played with the distance, and suddenly moved in to make a low hit on the thigh. My opponent lunged at the exact same instant, and I felt my epée snap with the force of his leg coming into contact with the point of my weapon. The resulting jagged end was so sharp that it went right through Granieri's fencing pants, made of extra strong protective cloth, and seemingly into his thigh, wounding him. He buckled over, dropped his epée and grabbed his leg; there was lots of blood all over, but, fortunately, it turned out not to be a deep gash.

A chair was brought over and Granieri made to sit down, while a doctor bandaged his thigh. The rule is that after an accident like this one, the wounded fencer is given twenty minutes to recover; if still incapacitated after that, he forfeits the match and, all other things being equal, the one who injured him is awarded the victory.

When his time was up, though, Granieri got back on his feet and after limbering up a bit, proceeded to get five straight touches against me to win the bout and move into the semi-finals. I was obviously much more shaken by the experience of wounding him than he was wounded: what if the broken end of my epée had punctured an artery and the Italian bled to death right there on the piste? I would have killed someone: a terrible thought!

But, as Coach Edo always said, in fencing, the head is more important than the legs.

IN THIS OLYMPIC year, the Canadian National Fencing Championships were held at the end of May in Saskatoon. As in 1972, this was also the final and the most important competition that would count in finalizing the selection of the Olympic team.

I fenced well in the first round, which was on the evening of the second day, the other weapons coming first, with the rest of the epée rounds, including the final, scheduled for the long third and last day of the competition. The semi-finals were a series of direct elimination pairings, with the first to get ten hits winning the bout. I was up against Rob Nichol, an excellent fencer from London, Ontario, I normally had quite a bit of difficulty beating; plus, he knew that he would make the team if he just finished in the top three since he had amassed enough points in other competitions. But this time, I fenced him impeccably and won ten to four. He must have been more nervous than I.

The final, though, was, as in the 1972 National Championships, very tight. At the end of the pool in which six fencers all faced off against each other, I was again tied with George Váraljay, the same Hungarian-Canadian fencer who had beaten me to go to München, and a young French-Canadian fencer, Alain Dansereau, each of us with three victories and two defeats. This time, though, I was determined to win the fence-off, and I beat both George and Alain quite handily.

I was the 1976 Canadian National Champion in epée fencing!

There was nothing now that could keep me from making the Olympic team, and indeed, my selection was confirmed by a telegram from John Andru the next day when I arrived back in Ottawa.

I had kept the vow I had made to myself in 1972.

THE OLYMPICS WERE still almost two months away, so we —those named to the team—intensified our training. When back in Ottawa, I worked out every evening at the RA, getting lessons from the local coach, John ApSimon and fencing against the other members of the club. In June, the Canadian Fencing Association organized a two-week trip for us to train in Paris at the elite Racing Club. The timing of this visit was unfortunate: because of the sweltering heat, the French went on vacation early. Indeed, the Olympic team happened to have two weeks of holidays before they went into their pre-Olympic training mode, and most of the fencing salles in Paris were closed. Nevertheless, we were trained by two young French coaches, Jean-Pierre and Jean-Michel, and fenced against the few second-tier French fencers who showed up at the Racing. There was not much time, though, to enjoy all that the City of Light had to offer.

AS IT TURNED OUT, I was not the only member of the family who would be at the Olympics that year. My sister, Clara, having just graduated from Harvard College four years after me, had been selected to be one of the hostesses for the Olympic Games. To look after VIPs. Having spent the previous summer at a camp in remote rural Québec, her French, that is to say her Québeçois, was fluent, plus, she also spoke Hungarian, and she was smart and good-looking.

Perfect for an Olympic hostess.

She and I were following in my grandfather's footsteps.

And in those of my paternal great-grand uncle, Dennis Wein, who had represented Hungary on the gymnastics team at the first Modern Olympic Games in 1896 in Athens.

I was proud indeed.

Chapter 6

The Games were set to begin on Saturday, July seventeenth, but the Canadian team formally occupied its quarters in the Olympic Village a week early. The press said this was to acclimatize ourselves. The coaches told us it was to get used to the venue at the University of Montreal and the routine of getting there from the Village in time for our events. And more importantly, for some last-minute training. A fine-tuning, they said. We, of course, were happy to be able to live and breathe the Olympic spirit for as long a time as possible.

We were not the only team to come early. Already on the first day all of us assembled in Montreal, after moving into our rooms, we went over to the Winter Stadium for an intensive training session. As we entered the huge hall that had been impressively set up with twelve fencing pistes dotted around on the floor, I immediately noticed that a couple of teams were already there practicing, also getting used to the venue. By the piste in the far corner, I recognized Iorgu, the Romanian fencer, standing beside a squat little man dressed in a warm-up suit watching two dueling athletes. When they stopped fencing and took off their masks, I saw that one of them was my friend, Paul Szabó. I was glad he was there because I was quite fond of him.

After warming-up and taking a routine lesson from Jean-Pierre LeCoz, one of the young French epée coaches the Canadian Fencing Association had hired after our Paris trip, I wandered over to where the Romanians also seemed to be taking a break. I asked Paul if we might engage in a practice bout or two. I was very familiar with the styles of George Váraljay and Alain Dansereau, my two epée teammates, and was glad to have someone new to fence against in training.

After three bouts, all three of which Paul won quite handily, we decided to have a break and chatted. Paul led me out of earshot of his teammates, coaches and the inevitable minders who were lazing around. We exchanged the usual superficial pleasantries, and since I saw that my teammates were starting to pack up to go to the showers, I was about to take my leave when Paul inquired, somewhat nervously, "Géza, I wanted to ask . . . would you know an address where I could have some money sent?" And glancing in the direction of the piste where his compatriots were, he continued, "A safe address. Friends of my family who live in New York said they would send me some dollars . . . "

I did not ask why, but I was sure that the Romanian athletes were allowed only a very little pocket money. Perhaps, for the Olympics, more than the five dollars they had been given to go to the Heidenheimer Pokal, but still, if anything, it would no doubt be a laughable amount.

"Of course, Paul. You can have them send it to me, care of my grandmother. She lives with my aunt in Dollard des Ormeaux, a suburb of Montreal. Probably a cheque is best; I can cash it and then give you the money." I was glad to be able to help, so I tore a corner off a score sheet that was on one of the tables and wrote down my aunt's address. "Here, just have them mail it here. To this address."

"Great. Thank you."

"In fact, it works very well. My sister is staying at my aunt's now too. She is a hostess at the Games and comes to work at the Olympic site every day. I can have her watch out for anything for you or me and bring the cheque or the notification when it arrives. Or whatever . . . "

I CALLED CLARA at my Aunt Klára's that evening and told her about Paul's request. She was glad to hear from me and ready to help.

The next day, the money question was a natural reason for Paul and me to repeat our training. This went on for the rest of the week before the Olympics started, and each time, unfortunately, I had a negative report for Paul.

No money had come. Nor even a letter.

THERE WERE MANY SOCIAL EVENTS around the Olympics, some of which we were also invited to. Such as the reception given by the Prime Minister, Pierre Elliott Trudeau, and the President of the Canadian Olympic Association, Harold Wright, to honour the members of the Canadian team. This was held at the Chalet de la Montagne on Mount Royal on the Wednesday evening before the Games opened. Trudeau showed up looking incredibly cool in a black leather jacket and an open-necked shirt, and he made the rounds trying to talk to as many athletes as possible. When it was my turn to shake the Prime Minister's hand, I wondered whether he would remember that we had met once before, in Japan.

That was when, on Canada Day, he visited the Ontario Pavilion at Expo '70 in Osaka where I was working, and the Commissioner of the Pavilion, General George Kitching, when he introduced me to the Prime Minister, mentioned that I had been instrumental in trying to help three Czechoslovak hostesses defect to Canada.

But I did not have the nerve to remind him.

THE OLYMPIC VILLAGE, which was made up of four triangular towers in some green space, was gradually starting to fill up as teams arrived during that week before the opening. It was a fabulous sight to see all these top athletes in their colourful training suits mingle at various sites in the Village or assemble at lunch or dinner in the cafeteria-style restaurant where we took all our meals. The food was delicious and healthy, and you could eat as much as you wanted. It was fun to mix with the athletes from other nations, an exciting experience to take your tray and sit down beside a stunning Amazon swimmer from Australia or a chic French participant in the equestrian event or a famous Jamaican track star. Or for that matter, any of these fantastic athletes. I felt very privileged to be there.

The other social venue was the Disco Bar, where some of the residents of the Village assembled to socialize. But on the evenings leading up to their events, most athletes did not drink or spend a lot of time there: it was mainly the coaches, officials and sundry denizens of the Village that went there for a beer. Only after our turn at competing was over, would we athletes frequent the Disco Bar.

UNFORTUNATELY, ALREADY LEADING UP to the opening, the Games of the XXI Olympiad became marred by political controversy. First, Taiwan pulled out, after Prime Minister Trudeau declared that the team could not compete under the name 'China.' Canada had initiated diplomatic exchanges with the People's Republic of China, and some of the conditions for that opening included giving up relations with Taiwan and restricting the use of the name 'China' to the PRC.

Worse still, during the week before the first day, sixteen African nations formally requested the International Olympic Committee to expel New Zealand from the Games because their rugby team was touring South Africa, which had been thrown out from the IOC for its apartheid policies. On Friday, the day before the opening ceremony, the IOC rejected this request, saying that rugby was not an Olympic sport and therefore the issue was beyond its jurisdiction. In the end, twenty-two nations from Africa, the Middle East and the Caribbean pulled out of the Games in protest and seven others would change their intention to take part after participating in the opening ceremony but before the first events.

SATURDAY, JULY SEVENTEENTH finally arrived: the day the Games of the twenty-first Olympiad were to open. A beautiful, sunny day. There was great excitement in the Olympic Village. After an early lunch, we wandered over toward the futuristic Olympic Stadium, 'the big O' as it had come to be known because of its purpose and its shape, or 'the big Owe' because of the debt that the City of Montreal had incurred for its construction. This centrepiece of the Olympic Park had already become a landmark in Montreal. Designed by French architect Roger Taillibert, it was still then unfinished, lacking its retractable roof amongst other features, but was undeniably an impressive sight even without these.

I remember lining up ten abreast with the Canadian team waiting for the opening ceremonies to begin and for us finally to march into the Stadium. We were all in our gaudy red and white uniforms, the men in red trousers, red-and-white striped shirt and white safari jacket, the women in white pants and red jackets, all decorated with little maple leaves down the side. We looked a bit like candy on sale to children at the fairground.

All eyes turned up to the sky when we heard the loud roar of jet engines as the Snowbirds, the famous squadron of flying aerobatic pilots of the Canadian Forces Air Command flew overhead of the Olympic Park performing their hair-raising stunts. This was followed at just after three pm by a trumpet fanfare to kick off the festivities inside the Stadium, and then a huge cheer when Lord Killanin, the President of the International Olympic Committee, and Roger Rousseau, the President of the Canadian Olympic Committee welcomed Queen Elizabeth, as the Head of State of Canada. She was accompanied by Prince Philip and their daughter Princess Anne, who was actually a member of the British equestrian team at these Olympics. Pierre Trudeau, the popular Prime Minister was there with his young and colourful wife, Margaret, as were Jules Léger, the Governor General and his spouse, Gabrielle, Robert Bourassa, the Premier of Quebec, Jean Drapeau, the Mayor of Montreal and his wife, Marie-Claire, and Roger Rousseau, chief of the Montreal Olympic Organizing Committee. The roar only abated as we heard a military band start up 'O Canada' and the crowd joined in the singing. After an interminable wait, we sensed that there was some movement up front, and then another loud cheer went up when the Greek contingent finally entered the Stadium, led by a wrestler carrying the blue and white Hellenic flag.

We had to wait our turn, while athletes and officials from the ninety-six countries who had stayed to participate in these Games marched into the Stadium, did a circuit of the track and lined up in the centre behind their national flag. But when Abby Hoffman, the middle-distance runner from Toronto, proudly carrying the maple leaf flag, led the first of the Canadian delegation through the portals, there was an unbelievable, deafening roar, wild cheering and clapping, that lasted until all four hundred and seventy-four athletes, coaches and other associated officials marched in and past the Tribune of Honor. I will never forget that feeling of stepping into a stadium packed with seventy-three thousand spectators, including dignitaries from all over the world, there for the pinnacle of athletic events. This is the high that the Greek athletes or the Roman gladiators must have felt performing in ancient times. And all the colours, wow, what a feast for the eyes: the flags, the uniforms, the streamers, the sky!

As I marched past the VIP box, I saw Queen Elizabeth, resplendent in a salmon pink dress and matching hat, occasionally supplementing her smile with her signature little wave. She and the other dignitaries stood for the entire march of the athletes in honour of them. Of us. I was one proud Canadian at that moment.

Once all the delegations were in the centre facing the Tribune of Honor, Lord Killanin gave a brief welcoming speech and requested Queen Elizabeth to open the Games. The moment, we, and the entire world had been waiting for, had arrived. There was a hush as the monarch got up and uttered the formalistic, but magical words: "I declare open the Olympic Games of 1976 celebrating the twenty-first Olympiad of the modern era!" Another deafening roar from the crowd was punctuated by the athletes throwing hats and other projectiles into the air.

Jean Drapeau, the 'punchy' little mayor, was given a huge ovation as he accepted the Olympic flag from Lord Killanin and the Mayor of München, the site of the 1972 Olympics. The banner was then marched around the track and hoisted by twelve athletes, all dressed in white. Pointedly, the twelve were all from Quebec, and some of them had just missed making the Canadian team, including two fencers whom I knew well.

The Olympic Flame was then lit by two young Canadian athletes, Stéphane Préfontaine and Sandra Henderson, reflecting Canada's bicultural heritage. It had been transmitted electronically from Athens to Ottawa, by means of a pulse derived from the perpetual flame burning in Greece, and then from Ottawa, runners had carried it to Montreal. A Canadian weightlifter, Pierre St.-Jean, gave the traditional Oath of the Athletes and an official, Maurice

Forget, recited the Judges' Oath, both in French and English.

A dream had become a reality, not just for me, but also for the other six thousand or so athletes standing there in the middle of the Stadium with me.

We were Olympians!

Chapter 7

The fencing events only started on Tuesday, July twentieth, the fourth day of the Games, with the men's individual foil event. Thus, on Sunday and Monday, we were still able to train at the University of Montreal facilities. But by this time, all the other teams had arrived and each team was allotted a time according to a strict schedule. When it was our prescribed turn on Sunday morning, I looked around but did not see the Romanians; I guessed that they must have been allocated a different slot. So I was not able to tell Paul that the money he was waiting for from his friends still had not come. Nor had any letter, according to my sister.

ON SUNDAY AFTERNOON, I had agreed to meet Clara over at the Forum. She was escorting Hungarian dignitaries to the gymnastics competition, where the Hungarian women's team was performing in the team compulsories in the same draw as the three other top teams: the Russians, the Romanians and the East Germans. I was keen to see the legendary Olga Korbut compete, after all, she had won three golds and a silver at München in 1972. The Russian woman gymnast had been seventeen then; now at twenty-one, she was up against some much younger girls.

When I arrived at the Forum, there was already a buzz in the crowd. I quickly found my sister with the Hungarian VIPs, who were laughing and backslapping each other, obviously pleased. Clara quickly explained that Márta Egervári, the star of the Hungarian gymnastics team, had earlier wowed everybody with a first routine on the uneven bars that scored 9.875. But then Olga Korbut on the Russian team, which had come next on this apparatus, had bettered her mark, with a 9.9. The girl now performing on the bars was the Romanian team's number two seed, Teodora Ungureanu. This little girl, only sixteen, seemed incredibly young to be a senior gymnast, but Olga Korbut, too, had been young in München.

Ungureanu did an amazing routine, for which she was also awarded a 9.9 by the judges. There was just one more gymnast to go, the Romanian top seed, Nadia Comaneci. The Russians had scored an aggregate of 48.85 in the compulsories, and Nadia needed to get at least a 9.75 for the Romanians to pull ahead in this discipline. Plus, in fact, she really needed to get more because the Russians had outclassed the Romanian girls on the floor exercises 48.70 to 47.55, and it was the aggregate score over all four disciplines that counted for the overall team gold. The pressure was on the diminutive Romanian girl.

Nadia gave her teddy bear a kiss, after all, at fifteen years, she was still just a child, but competing in the senior league before leaving the bench, and then turned to her coach, Béla Károlyi. Like Paul, a Romanian-Hungarian from Transylvania, Károlyi had recently been appointed head coach for the Romanian women's team. He now towered over Comaneci when he hugged her and gave her a last-minute word of encouragement.

Well, this little girl was unbelievable. She just flew over those bars, attacking them with immense strength and determination. A forward somersault over the high bar, releasing and just catching it, followed by three giant wheels, a straddle over to the low bar and then a perfect backward half-twist dismount. The elfin smile on her face as she skipped back to the Romanian bench to the wild applause of the crowd suggested that she knew she had performed an exceptional routine.

Her score took an inordinately long time to come up ... and then ... what's that? The electronic scoreboard indicated a 1.0. It can't be, a one? But suddenly the crowd began to clap, and even I realized that it was meant to be a 10.0. A perfect score! Unheard of, unbelievable! And then the announcer indeed confirmed that we had just witnessed the first routine ever given a perfect score in a gymnastics competition, and in typical Canadian fashion, extended the sincerest apologies of the organizers because the scoring system was only calibrated to show results up to a 9.975.

I looked over in the direction of the Romanian bench and saw that pandemonium had broken out, as all the athletes and officials were hugging Nadia. Not just the gymnasts, but as I looked closer, many other athletes who had come to watch their teammate. Including the tall epée fencer with the moustache, Iorgu. And then I saw Paul Szabó congratulate Béla Károlyi, his fellow Transylvanian.

I made my way over toward Paul and he finally saw me and came over to the edge of the crowd that had assembled around the bench.

"Wow! Fantastic! Congratulations," I could not find the right words. Other than the usual clichés.

Paul just smiled and said, "Yes, she was good."

"Paul, come and meet my sister. She's over there with the Hungarian team. And some of their brass."

So, as the Hungarian officials looked Paul and me over somewhat suspiciously—these Hungarian speakers who were not on their team—I introduced my friend to Clara, who was glad to make his acquaintance. She reluctantly confirmed to him that no money had arrived for him to my aunt's address.

"Thank you," Paul said, looking at the floor. "Hmm, it is possible that those family friends never got my mother's letter . . . I don't know . . ."

"Well, this is just the first day realistically anything might have come. There is still almost two weeks to go," I said, trying to give him some hope.

"Yes," Paul answered. But I could see that he was disappointed.

THE NEXT DAY, in the optionals, Nadia did even better, getting two perfect scores, in the uneven bars again and on the balance beam. It seems that the judges had decided that this little Romanian girl was a goddess in more than just one discipline.

She ended up with the individual overall gold, and gold medals in the uneven bars and the balance beam and a bronze in the floor exercise, as well as silver in the overall team results. Not bad for a fifteen-year-old.

But in spite of all her efforts, the Romanian girls had not been able to beat the Russians led by Olga Korbut and Nellie Kim in the women's team event. There were truly some exceptional young ladies competing.

TUESDAY WAS A BIG DAY for fencing. It was the kick-off day for the event, and our men foilists, Michel Dessureault and Tim Fekete, both from the RA, my Ottawa club, were leading off for Canada in the individual event, so we all went over to the Winter Stadium to cheer them on. The first round started at 8:00 am and George Váraljay and I targeted to get there just a little after.

We quickly checked on the roster and saw that Michel and Tim were in pools E and G, which were being fenced at the other end of the Stadium, so we made our way around in the stands to where we saw a pair of our women foilists, Donna Hennyey and Chantal Payer giving some strategic pointers to Tim, who was the youngest member of the team. We saw that Michel had already dropped his first bout 5:1 to the top-ranked Frenchman, Fréderic Pietruska, and Tim had lost 5:4 to the low seeded Hiknam Hossein from Iran. This did not bode well for Canada's fortunes in the individual men's foil event. Indeed, the two proceeded to lose their next bouts, and in the end, did not get out of the first round.

GEORGE VÁRALJAY, WHO had by now become a friend, and I had planned to stay at the Winter Stadium for the afternoon because the fencing part of the modern pentathlon was scheduled to take place. And I loved the pentathlon!

The five sports that it comprised, fencing, pistol shooting, horseback riding, swimming and running, were such different specialties and required quite disparate skills. It is rightly considered the most rigorous event in the Olympics, more so than the decathlon, even though that has ten events.

The modern pentathlon originated in the wish to bring together the disciplines that make a good soldier. Indeed, legend has it that the sport commemorates the brave feat of a young French cavalry officer in Napoleon's army. This soldier volunteered to deliver a message to Bonaparte, riding a horse he had never seen before. On the way, he was attacked by cavalry with swords and had to fence his way through, eventually shooting the soldier who had shot his horse from under him with his pistol. He then continued his mission running and finally, had to swim across a river to deliver the message. A wonderful legend and it gave rise to an amazing sport.

The fencing is done with the epée, the same weapon George and I fenced, with the difference that each bout lasts only one minute and whoever gets the first touch wins. Unlike in normal fencing, where usually whoever got the first five, or sometimes ten, hits, is the winner. Double touches are not counted, and if no one manages to score within the minute, then both competitors lose. The match is truly a duel and is based on the concept of first blood. Depending on the number of wins he or she racks up, the pentathlete is awarded a certain number of points. The competitor with the most points in all five disciplines wins the individual event and the team gold goes to the country with the best aggregate score for the three pentathletes who make up the team.

In fact, in 1972, when I was training with the Hungarian pentathletes in Budapest, I had come close to being recruited for the Canadian team, which was training in Hungary at the same time. I was clearly good at fencing, an excellent runner, and could hold my own at pistol shooting. I thought I could master a horse, but swimming was my downfall; I never did like the water.

Many of the Hungarian pentathletes I had trained with in Budapest were still on the team. Traditionally, Hungary had been a powerhouse at the sport, alternating with the Soviet Union in winning team gold over the last six Olympics.

But during the last few years, the Soviet team of Boris Onischenko, Pavel Lednev and Boris Mosolov had taken most of the titles in competitions since the team gold they had won in München. Boris Onischenko, a colonel in the KGB from Ukraine, had won the silver medal four years earlier behind András Balczó, the Hungarian, who was not competing in Montreal. Onischenko, now 38, or his teammate Lednev, who had, in fact, started to overshadow his Ukrainian teammate, had won many of the individual international competitions since then. Besides the Russians and the Hungarians, the Czechoslovaks and the Poles had individual medal contenders and a strong overall team, and the United Kingdom was considered to have an outside chance at a medal.

After horseback riding, the first event on Monday out at the Bromont Equestrian Center, the Soviets were in fourth place, 76 points behind the British team, which traditionally excelled at the equestrian discipline, but they were known always to do well in fencing which came next, and shooting which followed.

As we watched, George and I were thrilled by the ease with which Onischenko won five of his first six bouts. He only lost to Kancsal, the Hungarian, who was acknowledged to be an excellent swordsman. Next, the Russians came up against the British team. First up against the Ukrainian was Adrian Parker, the swimming and running specialist on the British squad. From where we were sitting, we could see that Jim Fox, the British captain, who had won bronze at the 1975 World Championships in Mexico City, approached as close to the piste as he possibly could, and crouched down to watch the bout carefully in preparation for his upcoming match against Onischenko. We were quite surprised that on the very first action, the green light lit up to show that Onischenko had scored a touch because we did not think that he had made a hit. There seemed to be some confusion on the piste, but the Ukrainian was awarded the victory. I saw Fox shake his head, seemingly in disagreement, and as captain of the British team, go over to Carl Schwende, an older Canadian, former fencer, who served as Président de Jury and whom I knew from the national fencing circuit. Probably to protest, I told myself, since he must have had some questions about the touch. As did I.

Onischenko won his bout against the next British fencer, Danny Nightingale, with a solid hit. There was no doubt on that one, and I saw Schwende glance over at Fox, who threw his hands up. In the next match, Parker lost to Lednev. Then it was Fox's turn against Onischenko. The wily old Fox played with the distance, seemingly wanting to trick the Ukranian into making an attack, while still being sure that he could avoid it. Onischenko lunged. Fox leaned so far back that the point was still at least fifteen centimetres from his body. Even so, the green light came on. George and I could not believe it, and we were sure that there had been no touch. Fox immediately protested, and the Président de Jury, having been primed by the British captain earlier, had to agree that something was amiss. He went over to confiscate the Ukrainian's weapon, but Onischenko obfuscated and tried to put the offending epée away and extract another one from his bag to give to the referee. However, Fox grabbed hold of the blade, and Schwende finally managed to get the suspect epée. He looked it over perfunctorily and then sent it off to the technical staff to be checked for a possible short circuit.

There were a lot of protestations from the Russians, and the Brits, too, were all over poor Carl Schwende. We all sat around dismayed, waiting for the report to come back from the technicians. Fifteen minutes or so later, I saw a man carrying an epée go over to the Chef de Jury, and explain to him what had happened. It did not take much more time for the buzz to get out: apparently, the technical specialists had found that the handle of Onischenko's weapon had a tight-fitting skin pulled over it, which, when removed, revealed a button that he could just depress with his thumb through the skin at will to connect the circuit and make the light come on for a touch. So he could pretty well always make sure the electrical judging mechanism registered the first hit in his favour. Gross cheating, clearly.

Colonel Boris Onischenko was summarily ejected from the competition. The Soviets appealed, since, with one of their stars thrown out of the Games, it would mean that they did not have the required three athletes to be eligible to finish competing in the team event. They were deprived of a good chance at not only the individual gold that they thought they had with Onischenko but also the team gold for which they definitely had been the favourites.

The Ukrainian pentathlete was whisked away in handcuffs, I think by his colleagues at the KGB, and taken to a Russian ship in Montreal harbour. As I later heard through the grapevine, the next day he was flown back to Kiev.

With the Soviets out of the running, and Hungary having performed abysmally in the riding event, the team gold was up for grabs. After the second day, the Czechoslovaks moved into the lead, and the USA was a surprising second, with Sweden fourth. A distraught Fox fenced terribly after his anxiety-producing encounter with the cheating Ukrainian and the UK slipped to eighth overall. Later The British team captain even said he had considered withdrawing from the event.

The third day, the day of the shooting, saw the Czechoslovaks strengthen their lead, and the Poles move into second place. The next day, in the swimming pool, Fox equalled his personal best time but it was still only good enough to place him thirty-fourth out of forty-six competitors. Parker, the swimming specialist, swam magnificently and the UK team moved back to fifth. Czechoslovakia was in first place four hundred points ahead of Poland, with the next three positions within two hundred points.

Thus, going into the fifth and last day, the three thousand meter cross-country run finale, it was still anybody's game. By the time it came to Fox's turn to run, the UK team had a remote possibility to win the gold. Fox, who was thirty-five years old, ran a phenomenal race but collapsed as he crossed the finish line and needed to be put on oxygen immediately. It took the judges almost half an hour to declare Britain the winner and Czechoslovakia second, with Hungary managing to pull up into bronze medal position.

This is the stuff Olympians are made of!

AT THE TIME, this Onischenko incident got a lot of press, and some editorials even raised the question of whether Onischenko's coaches knew about the rigged weapon and thus were party to the cheating. I doubted this because the Soviet and other Eastern European athletes my friends and I spoke to were very disapproving of the Ukrainian. For example, my friend Julie told me that one of the Russian women's volleyball team members had told her that she and her team members had agreed to push the dishonest pentathlete out the window if he ever came into their room.

What did indeed happen to Onischenko? Some early reports said that he was taken back in handcuffs to face jail in the Soviet Union. Some even said he was sent to the salt mines. Much later, I found out that he had apparently been called to appear in front of Leonid Brezhnev and given a personal dressing down by the President, then thrown out of the military, fined five thousand roubles, and stripped of all his past sporting medals. The same Los Angeles Times report had him working as a taxi driver in Kiev several years later.

But a fencing friend of mine who went to the Moscow Olympics in 1980, boycotted by both the Americans and the Canadians, as well as sixty-three other countries, because of Russia's failure to withdraw after invading Afghanistan, told me that he saw Boris Onischenko there as a member of the jury judging the fencing event of the pentathlon.

Stranger things have happened, especially when it comes to Russia. And the Olympics.

The truth though may have been lost with time.

ANOTHER PERTINENT QUESTION that some of us pondered was for how long had Onischenko's cheating been going on? Some time after he was caught, the officials looked back at his career over the previous several years and saw that at every major pentathlon event, he had won the fencing discipline, or at worst came in second. I, as a fencer, can attest to the fact that winning with such regularity is very, very difficult, if not impossible. Without cheating, that is.

But in the end, while I do not condone the cheating, I do understand why it happens. Onischenko and the other athletes from the Soviet Union and Eastern Europe had much greater pressures on them to perform than we in the west. For them, winning and staying on the team was the way to open the avenue to escape, at least momentarily, the repression, the want, and the drab life behind the Iron Curtain. This is, I think, also an explanation for the rampant use of drugs by some athletes from Communist régimes. But the pressure to win, to gain the glory of gold, is really what drives athletes, from whatever background.

How much better, though, to be remembered for a heroic win, such as that of the British team, led by Jeremy Fox, than to go down in disgrace and shame as did "Disonischenko"!

Chapter 8

Thursday, July twenty-second. Finally, the day of the individual epée event. It was to start at eight in the morning, so those of us competing for Canada left the Village for the Winter Stadium on the shuttle bus at just before seven. I was not feeling in top form, having slept only lightly and for just a few hours. Moreover, the coffee with cream and the pancakes with lots of butter and maple syrup I had eaten for breakfast to give me energy, was not sitting too well in my stomach as I clambered off the bus with my fencing bag.

Nevertheless, I changed quickly and got out on the piste to warm up with George Váraljay. I was not too happy that in the first round, as the number one Canadian seed since I was the National Champion, I had been put in pool A, up against Alexander Pusch, the top fencer from Germany, Giovanni Pezza from Italy and Bill Johnson, a very wily fencer whom I knew from the British Nationals, as well as an unknown competitor from Argentina, Juan Piran. A tough pool to be sure, but not impossible: Pusch was definitely out of my league, but with a little bit of luck I might beat

69

Johnson or Pezza, and should be able to win over Piran. And no doubt, all the pools were going to be tough: this was the Olympics, after all!

Things did not go my way, though. My fencing was sluggish, and while I did beat Piran, I lost to Pezza and Johnson, both of whom had risen to the occasion. And against Pusch, who went on to win the individual epée gold medal the next day, I did not even get a single touch. This, and the fact that Pezza and Johnson both made the semi-finals, did eventually console me later, but as I skulked on my way over to the changing room, I knew I should have done better. It was only a little after ten in the morning, and I was already out of the individual Olympic competition, what I had worked for and looked forward to for the last four years.

My Canadian teammates, unfortunately, did not fare much better.

As I looked up into the stands, I saw my family waving at me, beaming. For them, the fact that I had competed in the Olympics was already a major achievement. But I noticed that some of the friends who said they would come to see me fence had not even arrived! How embarrassing.

I resolved to put this behind me and do better in the team event several days ahead.

WHEN, AFTER SHOWERING, I came back out into the arena, I saw that some of the first round pools were still in progress. Including the pool in which my Hungarian friend, Kulcsár Győző, who had won gold in the Mexico Games in 1968, was fencing, and Paul Szabó's pool, both at the other end. I made my way there and watched Kulcsár's last bout against the top-seeded French fencer, Philippe Boisse, whom he devastated five to two, without too much effort it seemed.

On the other piste, even more exciting was the bout between Csaba Fenyvesi, the Hungarian gold medalist in 1972 and my friend Paul. As I looked at the scoreboard, I saw that Paul was having a great day, having won all his bouts until then, five to zero, five to one, five to one and five to three.

Fenyvesi, on the other hand, was not having such a good start, having lost a bout to another Frenchman, Philippe Ribaud five to two. In fact, Ribaud and Jurka, the Czech fencer who had managed to score three points against Paul, both had three victories. But Jurka's 22:17 ratio of "hits for" and "hits against" put him ahead of Ribaud's 20:17. To get into the next round, Fenyvesi could do no worse than lose to Paul five to four, which would give him a 21:17 ratio and put him in third place behind Paul, who already had four victories, and Jurka, with one more "hit for."

The bout was exciting and went to four four with the fencers getting alternate touches. In the end, Paul won five to four and was first, not only in his pool but, as the only fencer to win all his bouts, overall in the first round. A pretty amazing start for my friend.

Although I have no proof, and, at the end of the day, it does not really matter, I am quite sure that the two might have arranged the five to four win for Paul before the match since that would assure that they both moved on to the next round. I saw them exchange a few words before going out on the piste, and although I could not hear what they were saying, this could easily have been done quickly in Hungarian, which no one else could have understood.

Fenyvesi would then have notched up a debt to Paul that he would have to deliver on if Paul were ever in a similar situation. This is how fencing on the international circuit worked, I knew. But at this point, this was all guesswork, and Paul was truly fencing magnificently in the first round, so he deserved the win.

As I learned later, Paul had an exceptional pedigree as an epée fencer: three times national junior champion in Romania, a country with a population of 22 million, almost as populous as Canada at the time with 24 million, and three times senior, he was first selected to the national team when still in high school. Here, at the Olympics, he was only twenty-one years old, unusually young for this sport where experience normally counts for a lot.

IN FACT, MY TWO FRIENDS met again in pool A in the second round, but for both, it was their second bout, and after each having won their first one, the situation was not clear enough to warrant either absolving the debt or further deepening it. In the end, this round turned out well for the two fencers: even though this time Fenyvesi beat Paul five to two, to go up first from the pool with four victories, Paul also managed four victories and was second. At the end of the round, Fenyvesi was fourth overall and Paul sixth. Pusch was second and the six-foot-ten Swede, Rolf Edling, individual epée World Champion in 1973 and 1974, was first.

MY PARENTS AND SISTERS were still up in the stands, Clara had been given time off from her hostessing duties to watch her brother perform, so, after the second round, I went off to grab a bite with them. They were not at all disappointed in me and indeed, were very supportive and proud. In a side comment to me, Clara reported that still, no money for Paul had arrived at my aunt's.

I RETURNED TO WATCH the fencing, quite excited that at least my Transylvanian friend and the three Hungarians fencing in the individual event, Kulcsár, Fenyvesi and Osztrics, were all doing well and had made it through to the third round, the last twenty-four. I saw Paul over on the Romanian bench exchange some words with the head coach and then warm up with Iorgu, his teammate who had also made it through.

I watched Paul for a while, but he did not fence well, winning only two bouts out of five, one of these was against Bill Johnson, the Brit, almost as if to pay him back for having knocked me out. Johnson though, made it through to the elimination round of the last sixteen, whereas Paul was knocked out with a bad points-for-and-against ratio and ended up nineteenth overall.

The crucial bout for him too, was against Pezza, who had beaten me in the first round. It was four to four, and Paul was pressing him to the end of the piste. To me, and obviously to Paul too, it looked like the Italian stepped over the back line, whereupon normally, the referee calls a "Halt" and the offending fencer is moved back up one metre from the end and given a warning that if he steps over the line again a touch will be awarded against him. There was no "Halt" though, but to my horror, I saw my Romanian-Hungarian friend turn around and start to walk back toward the centre "En Garde" lines, as Pezza, in a very unsportsmanlike fashion, hit him in the back. The light, of course, went on, registering a touch against Paul, and the referee declared the bout in favour of Pezza, in spite of protests from Paul and the entire Romanian team.

Had Paul not turned around, he would have won the bout and gone up to the semi-finals. Who knows, he might have made the finals and perhaps even won a medal. He certainly was a good enough fencer. But gold medals are won and lost by such split-second decisions.

I tried to catch Paul's eye to console him and to report on the money situation, but he did not look up and hurried off to the dressing room. I understood, knowing how lonely and devastating defeat can be, especially when victory is almost at hand.

The three Hungarians, though, continued to fence extremely well, with Osztrics winning his pool and ranked number one after this round, and Kulcsár and Fenyvesi both making it to the last sixteen. The competition was slated to continue the next day, with the elimination matches in the afternoon and the finals in the evening.

BACK AT THE OLYMPIC VILLAGE, I was hungry, so after dropping my fencing bag, I went down to the cafeteria. I always enjoyed going to the dining facility, not just because the food was remarkably good and you could stuff yourself with all you could eat, but because of the colours of all the uniforms or sweat gear, the hustle and bustle of the athletes, coaches and other staff mingling there, speaking in a Babel of tongues, and the visible diversity of all the different nations that greeted me.

After I got my meal, Caesar salad, Lasagna and cherry pie, I looked around to see who was there that I might know. I was delighted to see that over at one of the tables sat Julie, the Canadian volleyball player with whom I had enjoyed the fling in Cuba, with several other members of her team surrounding her. I hesitated whether to go over or not, they would inevitably ask how I was doing, but my curiosity in how their team was faring, won out over my reluctance to broadcast that I was eliminated in the very first round.

"Hi, Jules! How are you guys doing?" I asked. "Mind if I join you?"

"Hello, Géza! Good to see you. Come sit here," the tall blonde said as she made room for me between her and a dark-haired Amazon. "This is Carla."

"Hi, Carla. What's up? Have you guys won any games?"

"Well . . . we lost our first match to South Korea. They were tough as nails. And you?" Julie asked the inevitable question.

"I'm out. First round. Had a tough pool."

"Shucks. Too bad. So sorry." And she put her hand on mine.

"Well, there's still the team event . . ."

As I said this, I looked up from my food and saw Paul enter the cafeteria. Alone. I stood up and waved to him to come and join us, and he acknowledged me with a slight nod.

"Do you girls mind if a Romanian-Hungarian fencer friend joins us?"

"No, but we're leaving anyway," Julie answered, glancing at the clock. "We have a tough game tomorrow morning. Against Brazil. Pre-game strategy session at seven-thirty. Early to bed. Coach's orders."

"Bummer. I was hoping to catch up with you at the Disco later."

"Nope, not tonight. Not till we're finished. A week today. If we get through to the last round, which we're planning to. That's when we can start to have fun again." And she blew me a kiss with a suggestive look.

The girls were already out the door as Paul came over to join me.

"What? Did I scare them away?" he said with a slight laugh. "The only reason I came over was to meet them. Especially the tall dark one. I liked her . . . from afar. They must be basketball players . . ."

"Wrong. Volleyball. But pretty cool all the same. Maybe someday I'll introduce you."

"So, we both had a bad day . . ."

"I did a lot worse than you. At least you got to the third round. But what happened, Paul? You were doing so well up until then . . . that bout with Pezza. Why did you turn your back, and walk away? Even if that idiot referee had called a 'Halt'."

"Well . . . I don't know. I just did . . . I thought . . ."

"Anyway, you did well."

"Man, I have been thinking how insane this all is. For us."

"What do you mean?"

"You know . . . before the last round, the stupid coach reminded us that Ceaușescu had promised each gold medal winner a car ..."

"Wow . . . that's quite something."

"Géza, do you know what a car means in Romania? Only high-level party members, those who have served the Communist Party well, have cars. Normal people can never get one. And here I was supposed to win the gold medal to get a bloody car!"

"That's not such a bad thing."

"As if winning a gold medal in the Olympics is not enough . . ."

"Sure, it would be a great honour."

"But also, what is not good is that by winning I would be supporting them. I would give those assholes more to brag about . . ."

"Yeah, I see what you mean. But still, Paul . . ."

"And then, to make it worse, that idiot, General Dragnea, you know, he is the head Securitate . . . what do you call it . . . 'minder' with the team, told us off in the locker room afterward for losing. Only Nicolae, you know, that jerk Iorgu, he praised, since he made the last sixteen. The rest of us, Popa and me, he said were not 'true patriots', and that there would be 'consequences' for us unless we managed to pull ourselves together in the team event later in the week. Threats like that . . . what an asshole . . ."

As Paul was talking, I couldn't help but think to myself that "Dragnea" sounded very much like "Dracula". But my gaze followed to where Paul's eyes had fixed on Iorgu and Popa standing at the end of the food line looking for a place to sit. They saw us and started coming in our direction.

"Oh, no . . . I wanted to ask . . . did the money come?" Paul inquired hurriedly.

"No, not yet."

"We'll speak soon again. Let's talk about something else for now.

Iorgu looked smug after topping his pool and making the last sixteen, so I reluctantly congratulated him and then said good-bye. I had never liked the guy and I did not want to tarry in his company.

He was a real creep. Probably secret service. Securitate.

Chapter 9

The next day was a big one for fencing. The first three rounds of the women's individual foil, as well as the elimination round and the finals of the epée. I got to the Winter Stadium around nine, and the first matches of the women's event were well underway. I was glad to spend some time watching the ladies; they were so much more graceful than the men. And the three Canadian girls, Donna Hennyey, the daughter of my former coach, Chantal Payer and Susan Stewart, had a better chance at performing well than any of the men.

In fact, Donna and Chantal managed to squeeze through to the next round, but in the end, they got knocked out there. Eventually, though, it was the twenty-four-year-old Hungarian girl, Ildiko Schwarczenberger-Tordasi who won gold the next day.

THE SEMI-FINAL EPÉE ROUND was one of direct elimination, with a repechage for those who lost the first time around, and it lasted almost four hours. My friends, Kulcsár and Osztrics, were among the six who made it through, as was

Pusch, the young German who had won my first round. The third Hungarian, Fenyvesi, the gold medalist in München, didn't. Nor did Iorgu. Nevertheless, the finals that evening were sure to be exciting, I told myself.

AFTER THE DIRECT ELIMINATIONS, I hung around outside the dressing room wanting to congratulate my two Hungarian friends who had made it through to the finals.

First out was Fenyvesi though. The one who didn't. He had officially placed seventh.

"Hey, Géza. Good to see you."

"Ya, sorry you lost, Csaba."

"Ahh. Doesn't matter. At least now I can go get drunk. And laid." I had heard that Fenyvesi was a legendary ladies man, even by Hungarian standards.

"Yeah," I muttered somewhat bewildered, as he started to walk away. Amazing, he was rationalizing away the chance at a gold medal just like that.

"Hey . . . say, Géza," Fenyvesi said, turning back to face me with a big smile on his face, "didn't you mention that you have your car here, my friend? I was wondering . . . could I borrow it this afternoon? Just for half an hour or so. There is a nice little Italian swimmer I'd like to bop. And you know how bad the rooms here are for that. No privacy." He obviously no longer had his mind on fencing.

"Ahem . . . sure . . . O . . . okay," I said, taken aback by the audacious, sexist manner of his request.

But I was not so sure.

Perhaps he sensed the hesitation in my voice because he started to negotiate. "I will give you some blades, Géza. However many you want. And . . . and penicillin, too, if you need some." This again confirmed a rumour circulating in international fencing circles: that Fenyvesi, as a bona fide doctor when not fencing, always had antibiotics on hand to ward off sexually transmitted diseases. For his own use, but he would be sure to have enough to supply his friends.

"All right then, Csaba. Come by my room, 324, at three, and I'll give you the key." In the end, I was a pushover. More for the blades than the penicillin, to be sure. Or just to please a former gold medallist in my sport.

FENYVESI BROUGHT THE KEYS BACK just before four-thirty with a satisfied grin on his face. And a dozen epée blades in his hand.

"Thanks. That was a lifesaver." I felt used, a bit like a pimp, but the almost three hundred dollars worth of quality epée blades, no doubt merchandise issued to the Hungarian fencer for free, certainly helped assuage my scruples.

"Are you going over to the finals now?" I asked, wanting to change the subject. "Or do you have to go with the team?"

"Naw. I'll come with you. They're all already there. Just let me get a bottle of Barack for Gyözö. He'll need it for sure. Meet you downstairs in five minutes." I assumed he was bringing the apricot brandy to celebrate if Kulcsár were to win, of which it seemed that he was perhaps a little too certain.

We got back to the Winter Stadium shortly after five, with Fenyvesi carrying a small travel bag slung over his shoulder, but instead of turning up the stairs to go into the stands, the Hungarian fencer headed for the dressing rooms. I followed him.

"Just a minute. I will get Gyözö to come out. Maybe Pista, too." Presumably, I thought, so I would be able to wish them good luck as well.

Several minutes later, Kulcsár came out with Fenyvesi. But not Osztrics.

"Szía, Géza. Come, have a good luck drink with us," Kulcsár said, as the two started walking towards the men's room. In the restroom, with no one in sight, Fenyvesi took a brown paper sack out of the shoulder bag and handed it to Kulcsár. A big swig, and then the bottle in the bag was handed around.

"Nothing like good old Hungarian apricot brandy before a match to put fire in your belly," Kulcsár said. "Here, have some more."

"No, you drink it. You're the one who needs it," Fenyvesi said, laughing as he handed the brown bag back to him. Kulcsár tipped it up and finished the contents. I looked on, with mixed feelings, amazed that these two would take the Olympic finals so lightly. Sure, I had often fenced with lots of alcohol in my blood after a night of heavy drinking, but I had never consciously gone out to get drunk right before a match. Especially the finals of the Olympics! Not that I ever had the chance. Or ever would, after my dismal performance.

Was Kulcsár just trying to add an extra element of difficulty? Of risk? Because, after all, the Olympic organizers had instituted random checks for drugs, and weren't all gold medalists tested? Perhaps Fenyvesi, the doctor, had something for that too.

Or was it simply that they had both already won enough Olympic gold? Between the two of them they had quite a haul: seven, to be exact, counting the team gold medals in 1964, 68 and 72 as well. But such a callous attitude, hard to believe.

"Good luck," I said, my eyes following Kulcsár wistfully as he went back in the dressing room. I made my way to the stands, troubled and perplexed, leaving a tipsy Fenyvesi with the team.

THE ATMOSPHERE FOR THE FINALS was electric. There was a raised piste down in the middle of the floor, and the Stadium was as full of spectators as I had ever seen it.

The announcer asked the audience over the PA system to be quiet for the introductions. The giant Swede, Rolf Edling, came out first, followed by the second German, Dr. Jürgen Hehn. The Europeans loved using their titles, although it amazed me how many doctors of something or other in fact there were among epée fencers. My friend, Dr. István Osztrics, a doctor of dentistry, included: he was introduced second to last. Before him came the Pole, Jerzy Janikowski, and Kulcsár, who looked a little under the weather to me as he almost fell when he tried to jump casually up onto the raised piste. I hoped that only Fenyvesi and I, who knew for sure what the reason was, had noticed his near stumble. The young Alexander Pusch, who had knocked me out in the first round, was the last to be called out.

There they were, the six Olympic finalists. What I would have given to be among them, there at the pinnacle of my chosen sport! But I had to consider myself lucky even to be here, to have competed in the Games.

The two Hungarians faced off first. I figured it was consciously arranged this way: in recognition of the fact that later in the match, the one might have thrown a bout to the other to allow him to win a medal.

Osztrics won the match five to three.

Their bout was followed by the two Germans: Pusch won easily five to two. As often in the finals of competitions of this calibre, no obvious winner of a pool could be pinpointed early on. Kulcsár beat Pusch but lost to Hehn. Osztrics, for whom I was rooting, since he was my 'countryman' and a really decent guy, beat Hehn handily, but lost all his remaining matches. After the last bout, the two Germans and Kulcsár, yes, amazingly, Kulcsár, in his inebriated state, ended up with three victories while the other three had two victories each.

If Osztrics had lost to him in the very first bout, Kulcsár would have won gold.

So Kulcsár, in his state, had clinched a medal. Where might he have ended up had he not drunk that half a bottle of barack pálinka?

A fence-off would take place to determine the order, but first, the three to fight for the medals were given twenty minutes to rest. Kulcsár draped the yellow bathrobe with the Hungarian emblem on it that all the Hungarians sported over his shoulders and sat down on the bench. I saw him take a drink from a plastic bottle, God, I hoped it was Gatorade, or just water, something non-alcoholic.

The two Germans fenced first, and the bout went to four hits each. The youngster Pusch waited for Hehn to attack, keeping his distance, and picked him off on the wrist when he lunged, scoring the winning touch.

Pusch's next bout was against Kulcsár. At 36, Kulcsár was the old man of the three, but I knew he was amazingly fit. He tried a few innovative moves, landed one. Pusch, however, was very quick and picked him off twice. Kulcsár's other two attempts ended in double touches: he was just that millisecond too slow. Maybe because of the barack pálinka, I thought. And then he seemed to give up, perhaps realizing that it was not to be: Pusch hit him with a beautiful flèche attack. Five to three. With the two victories in the fence-off, the twenty-one-year-old German from Tauberbischofsheim had won the gold medal.

There was still the silver to fight for. But by then, Kulcsár did not seem to care. Even though he was the better and more experienced fencer, he lost five to two to the other German. Oh well, he had added another bronze to his four golds and one other bronze.

Not bad for a booze-up, a fun outing. Which is perhaps how he would have looked at it.

Chapter 10

The team epée event was not until the twenty-eighth and twenty-ninth, three days before the end of the Games. George Vàraljay and I spent the intervening days watching our Canadian fencers in the other weapons events all go out in the first round, and practicing as much as we could in the specially provided training facilities. I regularly called my sister Clara or met up with her, but still no money had come for Paul. For some reason though, I did not bump into him in the cafeteria or anywhere on the grounds of the Village during all this time. However, if there had been some good news, I would, of course, have made the effort to seek him out. As it was, there was no reason to.

I did manage to make it to the Olympic Stadium to watch Hasely Crawford of Trinidad win the one-hundred-metre dash in 10.6 seconds, ahead of Don Quarrie of Jamaica and Valeri Borzov of the Soviet Union. And Lasse Viren of Finland captured the first of his two long-distance gold medals in a superb, tactical ten-thousand-metre run. I had loved track and field in high school, and I really enjoyed watching the events here.

But all the time I was trying to psyche myself up for the team competition which started on Wednesday. This could be my last major fencing appearance, I thought to myself. Although I had never consciously decided yet that I would give up fencing after the Olympics, I knew that I was not going to train as hard ever again. I was tired and ready to get on with the next phase of my life.

The twenty-eighth came around all too soon, and the team event started at eight-thirty. Which meant an early start: our coaches were determined to make sure we warmed up well. So we were there at the Winter Stadium by seven-thirty and were buoyed when we saw that we had drawn what seemed a comparatively easy pool. Placed in pool D, we had the Swiss to contend with, and we knew they were tough, having won silver behind the Hungarians in 1972 in München. Four out of five members of that team were here. Plus the Norwegians, who had some excellent fencers on their team too, but both these teams were now considered a notch below the Hungarians, the Germans, the Russians, the Swedes or even the French. And the last team in our pool was the Argentine, which we were confident we could beat. But to go up to the next round, we would need one other victory. Perhaps against the Norwegians, we might have a chance ...

Our first match was against the Swiss. Well, it was demoralizing. They fenced superbly and beat us thirteen to three. I fought terribly. My timing was off, and I was the only one on our team who did not even win one bout. All that training, all that excellent coaching and on the day when it counted, I simply could not put it together! I was ashamed, to say the least.

On the piste beside us, we saw the Norwegians beat the Argentines. Fourteen to two.

After a short rest, although we really did not deserve one after our dismal performance, we faced the Scandinavians. I still was not out of my slump: I lost my first three bouts but managed to win my last one. The only other victory we racked up was won by Michel Desserault, one of our foil fencers who had stepped in to round out the epée squad.

We were out of the team competition after another miserable performance. And that was it: the end of the Olympic Games for me. Probably, of my fencing career as well.

But we still had the Argentines to fence in the third of our matches. Here, at least we found a team we could beat: we tied them in wins at eight each and won because we had made two more touches than they. A Pyrrhic victory at best. It seemed that the South Americans were more our level internationally.

In pool E, next to us, I saw that the Romanians were going to advance after beating the Americans and the Thais, although they had lost to the Russians. Paul's record was also not stellar: he won only one bout against the Americans. That was, in fact, against my fellow All-Ivy fencer, Brooke Makler. And one against the Ruskis. It was clear that Paul, like me, was unable to surmount the 'dumps' and get into the right mental frame to fence well.

Before I left the centre of the Stadium, I wandered around to see how the Hungarians were doing. They were winning in their last match against the French, after having beaten the Poles and the Finns. So the team of Fenyvesi,

Kulcsár, Osztrics, Erdös and Schmitt was through to the next day's quarterfinals as well.

AFTER CHANGING, I went up to join my parents, other family members and friends in the stands. I felt again like I needed to apologize or at least say something to explain my dismal performance, but by the time I got to their seats, I found I had nothing to say to them. This was just one of those things in life, I decided: "you win some, you lose some". I had always been good at rationalizing failure. So I just muttered the obvious platitude, "Well, I didn't do so well ..."

I had lunch together with my family at a small bistro nearby and then I excused myself. I wanted to go back to the Olympic Village, to be by myself. And then later in the evening, to go to the Olympic Disco. To put it all behind me. To have some fun.

MY FRIEND PAUL SZABÓ signalled to me as soon as he saw me enter the dining room. He was alone by a window at a two-seater table, with just an empty glass in front of him. I went right over to join him.

"Hiya! I see neither of us fenced well today." I greeted him, having decided to put a jolly face on the matter.

"Yees ..." Paul seemed agitated.

"Let me just get some food."

"No. No! But Géza ... can we go for a walk?"

"I ..."

"No. Please, Géza. I want to talk to you. Not in here though ..."

"Paul, I wanted to tell you, the money still has not come."

"Come. Let's go outside." The information did not seem to register with my friend.

Once out of the cafeteria, Paul grabbed my elbow.

"Here, this way . . . Let's go over there." He pointed to a small grassy knoll to our left. "Back behind there."

I followed him. His long legs were moving fast as he glanced from side to side, scanning the surroundings.

"Paul, what's going on?"

"Here, let's sit over there." Paul climbed up the rise and then down the other side, a bit out of sight of most of the action in the Village, and stretched his six feet three inches out on the grass.

"I want to stay." When somewhat puzzled by what he might have meant, I did not answer, my friend continued. "After the Olympics. I want to stay here, in Canada."

"You mean . . . defect?" The enormity of what he was saying took me by surprise.

"Yes. I do not want to go back to Romania."

"Paul, are you sure?" I still could not believe my ears.

"Yes. I have made my mind up. I want to stay here."

Then it dawned on me. "Is that why you were waiting for the money?"

"No. No, that was not the reason. My mother asked her friends in New York to send some. So that I would have a few dollars to buy stuff with. But yes, it would certainly help if I had some dollars."

"Paul, don't worry. I will gladly give you some to get started if you stay."

"Thank you."

"But have you thought this through? You know, your parents will suffer back in Romania. No doubt they will be interrogated. Maybe . . . even . . . hurt." I wanted to be realistic, but I was treading on unfamiliar ground.

"Yes . . . I know. It is not easy for me to decide."

"You are sure?"

"Yes. That asshole Dragnea . . . you know the General. His comments keep coming back to me. That we are not patriots, because we did not fence well. And that there will be consequences . . . Do I want to go back to a country where they think like that?"

"Well, I see what you mean."

"You know, I didn't tell you . . . but at the end of each season, we all have to go to a big meeting. A session where we each do a 'self-criticism' in front of everybody else. The last time we did badly, my coach took the blame. 'I did not work hard enough. I let my country down. And so on.' He said stupid things like that. In front of the whole team. With his bosses sitting in the back and listening."

"Wow!"

"The saddest thing was that, afterward, I asked him why he said all those things. Why he humiliated himself like that. Do you know what he said? That if he didn't, his chance to get another star on his lapel would be gone forever."

"God."

"Do I want to go back to live in a place like that? A stupid Stalinist system. Where I would have to surrender my dignity . . . How crazy is that."

"I can see where you are coming from, Paul."

"And here . . . here . . . you have so much freedom. You can enjoy yourself without all that . . . all that crap to be afraid of. Canada is great."

"Yes, it has been good to my family, I can tell you that."

"My mother . . . I will miss her, I know. But I am sure she will understand. My father . . . I am not so sure he will."

"Will you still fence tomorrow?"

"Yes. But after . . ."

"At the end of the Games?"

"Yes. Please . . . but keep it secret."

A silence, while I gathered my thoughts to think through the consequences. And all that needed to be done if we were going to pull this defection off.

And he, his, as gloomier ideas must have been looming.

Then, out of the darkness: "Géza, tell me really . . . what will happen? Will I be able to go to university?" In his mind, he had already defected.

"Yes, I am sure. You will probably have to pass some tests. But I think teaching in Romania is tougher than in Canada. I skipped a grade when I started school here. Grade three." After I said this, it did not seem relevant.

"I don't speak good English . . ."

"But you speak French pretty well. You certainly had no trouble with the Québeçoise girls. And you will pick English up quickly, don't worry."

"It will cost money? University, I mean . . ."

"Yes. But don't worry. You will get assistance. And you can work until it starts."

"Will you help me . . . with all the arrangements?"

"Of course, Paul. We will drive to Ottawa. I have my car here. On Monday morning. You can stay with us, my friend

Mal and me. Tuesday, we will go see someone I know in the Department of Immigration."

A plan was starting to formulate in my mind. Gavin Stewart, the Canadian official who had tried to help me with the Czechoslovak girls at Expo '70 in Japan, was now back in Ottawa, a senior official in Immigration. He would help us, I was sure. And I could also seek Mal's advice when I got back.

"We will ask for political asylum for you."

"Thank you. Thanks a lot. You are a real friend."

"You would do the same for me." As an immigrant myself, whose family had escaped from Communist Hungary twenty years earlier and whom Canada had welcomed with open arms, I felt that it was my duty to help. Moreover, it was exhilarating to be engaged once again in a life and death game.

Just then three athletes, judging from their looks, I thought they were swimmers, female and East German, although I was not absolutely sure whether any of those qualifiers were right, turned the corner and came down the path in our direction. Paul saw them too.

"Let's go eat." Paul started to get up, disturbed by the three Olympians from behind the Iron Curtain.

"But not together."

"You are right, best probably not to be seen together."

"You still have a big day tomorrow, Paul. You go first. I will go back to the room and come down to eat later. But let's meet at ten tomorrow in the Disco. In the evening."

"Thanks again . . ." There was gratitude in his eyes.

And fear, at the path he had decided to take.

"Paul, good luck in the semis." And with the defection, I wanted to add.

But we were not there yet.

WAS I BEING MADE a fool of? Yet again? I could not help but wonder as I walked back to my room. No, surely not. I had known Paul for some time now, and I was positive that this was for real. He did not want to go back. And the situation in Romania, as it was starting to emerge in the western news, was pretty desperate. Despite all the bravado, all the fake news put about by Ceaușescu and his crowd.

I would help Paul.

AFTER COMMISERATING OVER DINNER with Peter Urban, one of our sabreurs, about how badly we had performed, he and I decided to go to the Disco. I was hoping that Julie, my volleyball player friend would be there.

She wasn't, nor were her teammates. But I saw my two friends, Scott Bozak and Brooke Makler, from the US epée team, knocked out in the first round like us, at the bar, so we went over to join them for a beer. The first one in a while: I had not had a drink since the Olympics began, although I had never given up the odd brewski or glass of wine while I was in training.

"There's Pop, the Romanian who just missed the individual saber medals," Peter said, halfway through the pint, as a dark-haired slim athlete came in with four other men. "He was fourth behind three Russians. Poor bugger, he just missed getting his car from Ceaușescu. Of course, the bloody Hungarians were nowhere."

"Well, you got two in the epée finals." Scott knew that both Peter and I had Hungarian backgrounds. "The Soviets got none. Nor did the Romanians."

"By the way, speaking of the Romanians, did you hear that two of their team defected yesterday?" Brooke asked, putting his glass down. "A rower and a canoeist."

"How?" I was intrigued. For obvious reasons. As I asked the question, I consciously checked to make sure that Pop's group was not within earshot.

"Apparently, they contacted some officials here in the Village. Security Guards or something."

"Yeah. Some Russians, too. A diver, and maybe others," Scott added. "Of course, I hear that both the Soviet and the Romanian authorities are putting pressure on you Canucks to give these defectors back. So they may not be with you for long . . . Poor buggers. Then they'll be really in for it!"

"Yeah. I heard the Ruskis are threatening to leave the Games. And to pull out of the Canada Cup next month," Peter said. "If we don't return them that is. Isn't that ridiculous?"

"Surely, you won't hand those poor suckers back!" Scott finished his pint. "I seem to remember that more than a hundred athletes defected in München. And the West Germans let them all stay."

"I don't know, this is Canada, man," Peter said.

"No, I'm sure we won't." I was trying to convince myself more than anything else. "This is a refugee-friendly country."

"Hey, Géza, do you remember the Olympics in fifty-six?" Peter asked.

"I sure do. Legendary. The entire Hungarian water polo team stayed on in Melbourne ... After winning the gold medal. And that famous semi-final game against the Ruskis."

"Infamous, rather. The 'Blood Bath of Melbourne'. That match went down in history," Peter explained for the benefit of our American friends. "The Games in Melbourne took place right after the Soviets entered the country to put down the Revolution. That's when we both left Hungary, too. The match had to be stopped one minute before the end. Pandemonium broke out after a Russian punched a Hungarian. I think it was Ervin Zádor . . . in the face and drew blood. This was after a lot of scuffling in the water, including the usual grabbing of testicles. Then the teams really duked it out . . . fans were jumping down poolside, several players were wounded and the water, in fact, started turning red. And since Hungary was ahead four to zero, in the end, they were awarded the match."

"They then went on to win the gold medal against Yugoslavia," I interjected.

"And then the entire team defected. Stayed on in Australia. But many of them ended up going to the US."

"Yeah, I read somewhere that, in fact, forty-eight members of the Hungarian Olympic team defected in 1956," I said. "Not just the water polo squad."

"Including most of the Hungarian fencing team," Brooke Makler joined in. "After winning two golds, a silver and a bronze. On that note, did you see, Béla Rerrich, who was on the epée team that won silver in Melbourne, is now here as the Swedish coach?"

"No wonder Edling was in the finals," I commented, as I got up to leave. "Rerrich must be a good coach."

With all this talk of defection, I was in turmoil, wanting to be by myself, not sure what to do. How to help Paul. As I left the bar to exit the Disco, I cast a glance at Pop and his group: three of them were short and stout, definitely not athletes, and probably not coaches, either.

Minders, then, I thought to myself? Secret police? The dreaded Securitate?

They sure were not letting their star saber fencer out of their sight!

Would Paul be able to get away?

Chapter 11

The next day was the last day of fencing: the epée team quarterfinals in the morning, followed by the semis in the afternoon and the finals that evening. The direct elimination quarterfinals started at the usual eight-thirty am, but I did not get there until an hour into the competition, having had enough of early starts.

Just in time to see Paul lose his third bout, five to two. Against the long-haired Swiss, François Suchanecki. The Swiss bench erupted in cheers, and I saw on the scoreboard that this gave them the all-important ninth victory to win the match. Paul had lost all three of his bouts. As he took his mask off, I saw that he did not seem to care: his mind was somewhere else.

Two pistes over, I saw that the match between Hungary and Norway was already over. Hungary had devastated the Norwegians eight to zero. Revenge for our loss to the Nordics, I told myself. A good start.

Romania next fenced Italy, another losing team, to determine eventual standings. Each of the Romanians, including Paul, managed two victories, which with their excellent touches for and against ratio was good enough for the team to win the close match.

That meant that based on the results, Romania would fence Russia for fifth place, Hungary versus Switzerland for third and Sweden versus Germany for first.

The Romania versus Russia match was first. The Russians dominated the Romanians, psychologically and physically. Paul won one of the only two bouts the Romanians managed to take, and that just five to four. After losing so badly, he and his teammates did not tarry by the piste and rushed off to the changing rooms. They ended up sixth overall.

Next, I watched the Hungarians fence for the bronze. What a disappointment! The Swiss were really on, but it seemed that the Hungarians just did not care. They managed only three victories against a team they should have beaten with ease, giving away the bronze medal. My hero worship for Fenyvesi and Kulcsár lost even more of its lustre.

Might they have been imbibing the apricot brandy again before the match? Based on past experience, not out of the question ...

DISGUSTED, I STARTED to leave my ringside seat, to go grab a bite in the snack bar, but just as I got up, I saw Fenyvesi come over.

"Hey, Géza. Gyözö and Pista and I wanted to ask you if you could drive us downtown tomorrow to buy some farmers. You know, to take back home with us." "Farmers" were what the Hungarians and other Eastern Europeans called blue jeans. His mind was definitely not on fencing.

I didn't have anything planned for Friday. But I was disappointed in my erstwhile heroes and was not sure that I wanted to help Fenyvesi and his friends buy blue jeans to smuggle into Hungary. Because that is clearly what this was all about. I had already tarnished my moral scruples by lending Fenyvesi my car for his romantic interlude with the Italian swimmer.

"Sure. What time?" So what, in the end, I thought to myself. It would be something to do, and an outing with the Hungarians could be fun. Plus, I wouldn't be seeing them for a while after the Olympics. Moral scruples be damned.

"How about the afternoon?"

"I was thinking of going to see some track events then …" Still, I did not want to give in too easily.

"Well, could we do it in the morning? Would ten be okay?"

"Fine. Meet you in front of the cafeteria." In the end, I was a real sucker.

I GOT BACK to the Winter Stadium in time to get a good seat to watch the finals, which were to start at six. Between the Germans and the Swedes. The Germans were favored, as they had taken gold and silver in the individual. But the Swedes had two superb fencers to match Pusch and Hehn, the giant Rolf Edling and the incredibly fast Hans Jacobson.

Plus, a great Hungarian coach, Béla Rerrich.

Indeed, it was the underdog Swedes who prevailed that evening, eight to five, to win the team gold medal.

SINCE NONE OF "MY" TEAMS had won a medal, I did not wait around for the medal ceremonies to finish. Moreover, I wanted to make sure that I was back in good time for my rendezvous with Paul at ten. In the Disco Bar.

In the dark of the shuttle bus, I thought to myself that maybe the Disco was not such a good place for a meeting after all. Judging from the three goons that had hovered around Pop yesterday. Oh well, I thought, we can always go and talk outside somewhere. All we need is a quick exchange on the dance floor or at the bar to arrange it.

"HI, JULES," I yelled in her ear above the music as she was sitting at the bar with her friend Carla. "Where ya been all my life?"

"Where have you been? We have been coming here every night since we were knocked out five days ago ... By our Cuban friends, of all teams."

"Well, the fencing just finished today ... Hi Carla!" I looked beyond Carla in search of Paul. Not here. "Can I buy you, girls, a drink?"

"Carla wants to meet your friend. You know, the tall handsome one from the cafeteria the other day."

"Oh, Paul? Paul Szabó? He's a Romanian-Hungarian fencer. I was supposed to meet him here tonight." My eyes continued to scan the bar for Paul.

"We haven't seen him."

I danced for several gigs with Julie, then with Carla. I was on my fourth beer, the girls had had quite a few gin and tonics, and still no sign of Paul. In fact, no Pop, no Romanian fencers.

"Hey, let's go look outside. Maybe my friend wanted to stay out of the smoke," I suggested, tired of the noise and the filthy air, and wondering what had prevented Paul from coming.

Gosh! Maybe it was those defections. The minders were probably keeping a very close watch on the entire team now.

We wandered around the Village, and I looked everywhere, including on the grassy knoll where we had had our discussion the day before, but there was no sign of Paul. Perhaps, I should have come outside sooner.

"Sorry to disappoint, Carla. If I see my friend, I will tell him that you were looking for him."

"No. No. It's okay. I'm going to turn in. See you guys."

I was glad to be alone with Julie. We strolled back toward the rise, and up to where Paul and I had sat to talk about his defection. We stretched out on the grass, kissed and made out in the dark. This, too, I had missed since before the intense days of the Olympics and the lead up to it.

There were going to be many benefits from returning to a normal life.

Chapter 12

The next morning, I lingered in bed until nine o'clock, wanting to leave just enough time for a quick breakfast before meeting the Hungarians for the jeans expedition. I got down to the cafeteria after nine-thirty still bleary-eyed and hung over. I lined up with my tray and picked up a stack of blueberry pancakes and bacon, juice and coffee and looked around to sit with someone. From his usual two-seater table over by the window, I saw Paul making agitated signs for me to join him.

"Paul, where were you last night?" I asked as I slid into the seat across from him. "I was waiting for you at the Disco. So was a hot chick. That Canadian volleyball player. You know, Carla, the dark-haired one who left just as you came over the other day. "

"I couldn't get away."

"What do you mean?"

"Some members of the Romanian team disappeared. They won't tell us what happened, but we all think they defected. They are not letting us go to places where we can meet westerners now. Except to the cafeteria."

"Ya, you gotta eat."

"Even here, they want us to come with someone . . . But I just sneaked out."

"Paul, I don't have much time this morning." I was shoving my pancakes down as fast as I could. "Let's meet tonight. At seven. Dinner time. Right here. Do you think you can get away?"

"Yes. I will try. I want you to tell me what will happen if I stay . . . "

"We can talk about that and how we will do it, tonight. Okay?" I got up and picked up my tray. Through the floor to ceiling windows, I saw Fenyvesi, Kulcsár and Osztrics approaching from their building. Even though I knew it was not rational, if possible, I did not want them to see me with Paul.

"Okay. See you then," Paul said hurriedly. I could see, though, that he was not too happy. But I couldn't figure out how to put off my Hungarian friends. "If I cannot be here at seven, wait an hour. Please. Or if that doesn't work, let's meet tomorrow morning at nine."

We were running out of time. As I went out to meet the almost-bronze medallists, I kicked myself for agreeing with Fenyvesi to do the jeans expedition.

It was a beautiful Montreal summer morning, and with the competition behind them, albeit with somewhat disappointing results, the Hungarian epéeists were even more relaxed than usual.

"Hey, Géza tell me, how much do you rent your car for?" Osztrics asked as we left by the South Gate in the direction of my car. "The screw mobile, I mean," he added with a laugh. "How much?" So Fenyvesi had bragged of his exploit with the Italian babe.

"For you, special price . . . Only one hundred blades an hour . . ." Osztrics laughed as I continued: "Today is real bargain. Only one hundred forints. I take you to buy . . . farmers. But no making out in the back seat with Csaba . . ."

I drove the three of them to a blue jeans wholesaler in the Garment District that I had found in the Yellow Pages. Well, these grown Hungarian Olympic medallists were like kids, rummaging through all the blue denim apparel.

"Seven dollars! Great price for farmers," Kulcsár said at the cash register. "We can sell them for a hundred back in Hungary."

They loaded up on Levis at seven dollars a pair, the trunk of my car was filled with blue jeans and there was even a stack of them between Osztrics and Fenyvesi in the back seat. Jeans blocked my view through the rear window.

"Can you stop at a luggage store?" Kulcsár asked.

"Good idea. I was wondering how you will get all your farmers back to Hungary."

They each got a huge suitcase, and we stuffed them full of jeans. But there was still denim left over, crammed in every nook and cranny of the car.

"We will pack the rest in our fencing bags. What equipment we have left, you can have, Géza," Osztrics said. I had thought they had already sold most of their fencing gear to finance the purchase.

"We will have to give the customs officials more pairs than usually," Fenyvesi said to his teammates as we headed back toward the Village. "Except you, Győző. You won a bronze." They explained that the unwritten rule was that the customs officials would look the other way if the team brought back medals; if they didn't, it would cost them in bribes. In kind, usually, because everyone knew the game.

BACK AT THE Olympic Village, I helped the Hungarians carry the loot to their rooms, and walked away with several masks, epées, blades, cords, two brand new fencing gloves and other assorted equipment. I ended up doing well too because my hoard was worth several hundred dollars. Not forints. A mutually beneficial morning—unless, of course, my Hungarian friends got detained at the border. But that was their problem. I was confident that no one in Canada would know or care that I had been rewarded by my friends with contraband stolen from the Hungarian state.

After depositing the goods in my room, I went to the cafeteria to grab a quick bite, looked around for anyone I knew, and not seeing anyone, hurried over by myself to the Stadium where the track and field events were still in full swing.

The stands were packed, and it wasn't just because it was a gorgeous day. Lasse Viren was running in the five thousand meters, and although the Africans had withdrawn from the Games, he was up against some good runners who could still prevent him from taking the double. For the second time. Because he had already won Olympic laurels in the five and the ten in 1972 in München, and the gold was his here already in the ten thousand meters.

This was another tactical race, but Viren was the master of tactics. He pulled away from the competition in the curve to win by several meters over Dick Quax of New Zealand. Only to announce right after that he felt so good that he would run the marathon the very next day. Never having run a marathon before.

And then I was glad to see the one and only Bruce Jenner complete the last events of the decathlon, to break his own world record and to win the gold medal. There were other thrilling events, and I thoroughly enjoyed lazing away the afternoon in the Stadium. It was sheer joy not to have to worry about the next competition, the evening's training session, maintaining my form. I think it was the only time I ever ate 'poutine', the very unhealthy French Canadian staple of french fries, doused with melted Kraft cheese and gravy, and spoiled myself with two beers.

Time to let myself go a little.

I SAW PAUL already through the glass wall as I approached the cafeteria. He was at the same table with just a glass of water in front of him. I knocked on the pane and signalled for him to come out, and started walking toward our favourite place on the back of the grassy knoll. By the time he finally sat down beside me, I had already stretched out on the grass, distracted by thoughts of Julie and the previous evening.

"It was difficult to get away. I had to tell them I was going to the clinic. For some medicine."

"Will they check?"

"I did go there. Got these." He pulled out a package of Imodium.

"You told them you had diarrhea?" I laughed.

"Ya. Don't laugh. I do have it," Paul countered defensively. "From the stress. All these stupid Communist games . . ." And then after a pause, he added, "Géza, I am afraid."

"Don't worry. I have thought about it. I have a plan. It will be easy to get away from here that is."

"How do you think . . . how do you see it? "

"Monday morning, I will tell you where my car is parked nearby and you simply take a stroll there. You should just leave your stuff on the corridor in front of your room, so no one sees you taking it with you. That could lead them to think that you are saying goodbye and leaving. Don't worry, I will bring it out. We will then drive to Ottawa, and I will take you to see the officials who will arrange to grant you asylum."

"And then?"

"Of course you can stay with me. With us." I was thinking already of the cottage Mal and I were renting. I was in one of the little cabins, but there was still another empty hut that Paul could have. "And I will give you some money to get started. You will have to work hard, though, you know."

"Will I be able to go to university?" This seemed to be his main concern.

"Yes, Paul. I am sure you will get in. But your life won't be easy at first. Have no illusions about that." I wanted to paint a realistic picture.

"Do you think I can become a psychologist?"

"Well ... yes ..." Paul was getting way ahead of himself. I had to slow him down. To focus him somehow. He had to get through that gate first and over to my car on Monday morning, without the Romanian goons tugging at him.

"And my parents? What will happen to them?"

"Paul, you know better than I. They will likely . . . "

"I can't do it ..." Paul jumped up suddenly.

"But Paul ..."

The mention of his parents must have had an effect on him. "I have to go back." He started down the hillside but glanced back. He had a tormented, pleading look on his face. "Géza, let's walk . . . I can't . . . I just cannot sit still."

"Paul, I thought you had made your mind up . . . "

"I will never see my mother again if I stay. My father, too. "

"I don't know, but over time . . . maybe . . . " I did not want to tell him that my mother never saw her father again after we left Hungary. And that it was for the same reason that in the end, my Czechoslovak hostess friend, Zozana, didn't defect in Japan; as a ploy, she had been told that her mother had cancer and she was afraid she would never see her again.

"No. I will do it. Come to think of it, I am sure my mother would not be against it. She would be happy for me to have a better life here. In freedom . . ."

Back and forth. Yes and no. Poor Paul, he was obviously struggling. Not wanting to let go of the past, to leave the loved ones behind. I did not want to paint too rosy a picture, but at the same time, I wanted him to realize that here, in the Free World, people have options. And opportunities. But also, that they have to work hard to make something of them.

We wandered around the Village several times while Paul wrestled with the known and the unknown. I tried to act as a mirror, throwing back the questions at him. In the end, he was the one who would have to make his mind up.

Come what may, I could only help him execute a plan and ease into a new life if he did end up wanting to stay.

Before we parted that evening, we agreed to meet the next morning at eight for breakfast. That would give him enough time to make the final decision. It would be a sleepless, tormented night for my friend, of that I was sure.

Chapter 13

The next day, Saturday, was the last full day of the Olympics. Sunday would conclude the Prix des Nations equestrian competition, the very last event, and then the Games with the evening closing ceremony.

But first, there were still some exciting track and field events to watch. Despite the steady rain, I hooked up with Julie and Carla to go over to the Stadium. I wanted to be there for the thrilling finish of the marathon, with my hero Lasse Viren running against Frank Shorter, the American winner of the gold in München.

While we waited for the marathoners to make it through the wet streets of Montreal, there was the excitement of the high jump finals. This had been my best track and field event in high school, and I loved watching the sport. All the more so because two excellent Canadian jumpers had qualified among the last fourteen, Claude Ferragne, the home-grown Québec favourite and Greg Joy, from British Columbia. Canada had a solid chance for a medal in this event.

But it would be tough, because the local boys would be up against Dwight Stones, the American who held the world record and had taken bronze in München in 1972, as well as a very tall twenty-year-old Pole, who had won the European Junior Championships in Athens the year before and seemed to be on a roll, as well as a number of other excellent jumpers.

Stones was not liked in Canada. He had been in an unfortunate altercation with a French-Canadian official in a pre-Olympic competition in Montreal earlier that year which had earned him a reputation as a prima donna. He complained vocally in the press about the cramped conditions and the lack of spirit in the Olympic Village, and took issue with the incomplete, roofless Stadium, singling out the responsible French Canadians as "rude". This was interpreted by the Québeçois press as an insult to French Canadians, whereupon Stones left the Village in a huff to go back to California to prepare for his event which was scheduled to start on the second last day.

When he came out for the finals, the crowd booed him, a contrast to the loud cheer they gave Ferragne and Joy and the muted applause for the other competitors. The jeering continued until he took off his 1972 München warm-up jacket to reveal a T-shirt underneath that said 'I love French Canadians' on the front in big bold letters. Seeing this, the crowd did give him a cheer; after his first jump, the officials, however, made him take it off and jump in the official 1976 US team gear.

Of the fourteen jumpers who had qualified for the finals, two went out at 2.14 metres, including Bill Jakunis, who had actually beaten Stone at the US Olympic trials. Wszola passed until this height, but cleared it on his first jump, giving him an advantage over all the other jumpers. The bar was raised to 2.18, and just then it started to rain. This height knocked the third American, Jim Barrineau, and the French-Canadian, Ferragne, out of the competition, leaving still ten jumpers to continue.

The bar was moved up to 2.21, and by now the rain was coming down hard. Stones, who was known to not do well in rainy conditions because of the speed and aggressiveness of his run-up, jumped first and cleared the bar. Greg Joy also succeeded on his first attempt, while Sergei Budalov, the Soviet National Champion, made it on his second. Everyone else failed at this height.

With only four jumpers left, the competition had now become interesting. Wszola and Stones had no misses up to this point, but the young Pole led because he had taken fewer jumps to get here. Joy had a total of three misses at various heights but was in third place since he had taken only one try to get over 2.21, while Budalov had needed two, although he had no misses at the lower levels.

As the bar was raised another two centimetres to 2.23, the conditions were tangibly changing for the worse but this close to the end of the Olympics, there was no question of postponing the last few jumps. It was so bad that water was collecting in pools in the run-up area, and officials came out with "squeegees" to try to mop it all up. Stones picked up a rag too, as did the other contestants. The soaked spectators who remained in the stands made very little noise as they watched the unusual proceedings down below.

Except when Joy finally took his first jump. But he missed his first try, as did Budalov. Stones desperately tried to mop up the water again before his attempt, but ran right through the bar, grabbing it with his hand. Jacek Wszola cleared this height on his first jump. Tactically, going for the gold, Budalov passed on his next try. Stones made another feeble attempt, but failed, ending his chances for gold.

Attention turned to the local favourite. This was Canada's last chance to get its first gold medal at these Olympics. So the crowd was ecstatic when he cleared the bar with his last jump, moving into second place.

On to 2.25. Wszola missed on his first try. Here was the Canadian's chance to take the lead. But alas, he, too, missed. As did Budalov. On the second attempt, the Pole managed to clear the height. Seeing this, Joy passed, since he knew it was not good enough for the gold if he just matched Wszola. Budalov missed again, so with only two jumpers left, Joy had clinched the silver.

The bar was raised to 2.27 since Joy still had two jumps left, and Wszola three at the new height. The spectators were hushed for the Canadian's first try, and there was an audible collective groan when he missed. The Pole, too, missed. The second tries were no more successful for either jumper. Joy had the silver, recording a personal best. The Pole was the winner of the gold medal, and with the clearance at 2.25, he had set an Olympic Record. The competition ended with an anti-climactic, failed attempt by Wszolak at 2.29 with his last try. Stones had the bronze, but as the World Record holder, he must have been deeply disappointed. With the rain still pelting down, the crowd gave all the competitors a standing ovation.

BACK OUT IN THE STREETS, Shorter led almost from the start. But it was a well-known fact that he, like Stones, hated competing in the rain. He was the favourite although with Viren's two medals, everyone was pulling for the Finn to repeat the Czech Emil Zatopek's incredible feat in Helsinki in 1952. A buzz went up in the stands as we all could see on the big screen that at the twenty-five-kilometre mark Shorter was passed not by Viren but by a runner no one had ever heard of before, Waldemar Cierpinski of East Germany. Cierpinski powered past Shorter and was first to enter the Stadium. Instead of the standard one lap, the East German did a second four hundred, just to be sure. Shorter followed into the Stadium fifty-one seconds later to get second. Viren managed fifth, but even that, after two golds in the five and the ten thousand, was an incredible achievement.

Perhaps even greater than the unknown Cierpinski's, as it turned out many years later. Files uncovered in the Stasi archives in 1990 implicated the marathoner in East Germany's doping scandal, confirming Shorter's suspicions at the time. The US sought to have Cierpinski's gold medal win annulled, along with the sweep of medals by the East German women's swimming team, on the grounds of doping, but to this day, the results have not been altered.

My then hero, Lasse Viren, has since also come under suspicion for blood doping.

It is sad that the pinnacle of sports achievement has become so tainted with cheating.

Better then to lose and maintain one's integrity. After all, the Olympics are really about competing, about being there.

Winning is another matter. But for some, it is all.

Back in the Olympic Village, I had dinner with Julie and Carla, and I kept looking around for Paul. We took our time to eat, all the while hoping my friend would show up. He did come, just as we were finishing our dessert of blueberry pie and ice cream, but not alone. He was in the company of Iorgu and Popa and three other men who were short and stocky, and therefore might have been coaches, but were more likely to be minders. My eyes met up with Paul's, but it was clear that he would not be able to join us. Given the disappearance of two of his teammates, there was no chance he could hive off from the Romanian group and talk to a group of Canadians. Too bad, because this would also have been a good time for him to meet Carla.

We would have to resort to the backup plan, to meet the next morning over breakfast at eight. We were cutting it rather close, but what could we do?

I left with the two girls and we agreed to meet again at nine in the Disco. I was beginning to feel nostalgic: the Games were rapidly drawing to a close, and there remained only tonight and tomorrow to experience the life of an Olympian. After that, all these amazing athletes would return to their countries, most to start training again after a brief rest, some like me, to quit and start a new life. And a few, like Paul, to really start a new life in a new country. I had to make the most of this while it lasted.

When I got to the Disco, the bar was already quite packed. Others were no doubt feeling the same nostalgia. Of course, the Hungarians, inveterate partyers, were all there, spiffy in their new Levis. I gravitated toward them, and Osztrics bought me a beer.

Julie and four of her friends from the volleyball team, including Carla, arrived around nine-thirty. They came over to where I was standing with my drink, and I introduced them to the Hungarians. I made it clear to the fencers in Hungarian that Julie was off limits. Fenyvesi immediately started chatting Carla up. Poor girl, I thought to myself, thinking of the penicillin Fenyvesi carried around. Too bad Paul had missed meeting her: who knows what might have developed? Possibly more than a one-night stand, as would be the case for Carla if she went off with my friend Csaba.

Julie and I danced close and could not keep our hands off each other. Nor our mouths separated. After four or five beers, the physical attraction was such that I could stand it no longer. I pulled her toward the exit to go outside.

We started heading toward the usual spot on the grassy rise, but halfway there I changed direction.

"Let's go to my room," I whispered in her ear. "I'm sure the others will all be out celebrating." I did not want my three roommates there when I arrived with my volleyball player friend.

Fortunately, my hunch was right. As soon as I pulled the door to, Julie and I were at each other, kissing and madly pulling each other's clothes off. I guided her over to my narrow single bed, and we hurriedly made love. It was not very satisfying, but necessary.

We did not dare linger long, for fear of one of my roommates walking in, so we went back to the Disco. But neither her friends nor the Hungarians were there anymore. This did not bode well for Carla, even though Fenyvesi did not have access to my car. After a few dances that seemed anti-climactic, we both decided it was time to go and turn in. A good night kiss later, and I was alone, somewhat relieved, but feeling a little empty.

Was this ultimately what Olympians experienced?

Chapter 14

The next morning, I was a little hung over, but after a quick shower, hurried to get down to the cafeteria. It was a beautiful Montreal summer morning: the sun was blazing and there was not a cloud in the sky. Paul was already sitting there in his usual spot by the floor to ceiling window. He looked like I felt.

"Sorry. I could not get away yesterday."

"Too bad. I had Carla, the gorgeous volleyball player lined up for you."

"Could they send me back?" Paul's mind was obviously somewhere else.

"Yes. Maybe, but not likely." I switched into defection mode.

"And then . . . if they do . . ."

"Well, they may give you a hard time. As far as I know, the Czechoslovak girls I tried to help in Japan who went back were not able to continue their studies, or else lost their jobs."

"No . . ."

"Paul, you were also in the army, weren't you?"

"Yes. I was a Sergeant-Major."

"They may say you tried to desert."

"I could be court-martialed. Desertion is serious in Romania . . ."

"Whew, Paul. That's not good." I was starting to get concerned. This put matters into a different league.

". . . I could be shot."

"Don't worry. You will not be handed back." I was trying to convince myself too.

"Are you sure?"

"Paul, we will leave tomorrow." Better to focus on moving forward, I told myself. "Meet me here at nine."

"I am not sure. It is too risky. Not just for me. For my parents, too. I don't know what will happen to them. Or to me."

"Paul, yes, it seems dangerous now. But probably a lot more than it really is."

"What do you mean?"

"For sure, if you do succeed, you will have a much better life." Concentrate on what he will gain by staying. "And you will be able to help your parents. Send them money. You will forget about how risky it was."

"Don't be stupid. I won't be able to contact them for years. If ever."

"Well, you have to make your mind up by tomorrow." My headache was getting worse. I was starting to lose heart too. It all seemed to be coming apart, right at the last minute.

"We have run out of time, Paul. If you want to stay, I will help you."

"I am not sure . . ." Paul looked out the window to avert my eyes.

"I will come back here at nine tomorrow morning and we will drive away if you want. If not, we will just say goodbye. Part as good friends. How about it?" We had to "shit or get off the pot" as my friends in college used to stay. No more vacillation, undecidedness.

"Okay . . ."

IT WAS A DAY for everyone to pack and get ready to leave. The closing ceremony was later that evening and, of course, we all wanted to be there for it. It was sure to be a giant party, a celebration of the last two weeks. No, the last four years. Of our lives.

After a hearty early dinner, spiffily dressed in our uniforms, we wandered over to the Stadium for the start of the seven o'clock closing ceremony. Those of us not participating later in the official march of the athletes into the Stadium, reserved for six selected athletes from each country, gathered at one end of the already full venue. We were given a huge cheer when we walked in. A party atmosphere reigned, and athletes were cavorting, chatting to hostesses, security staff, even spectators reaching down from the stands. Some members of the crowd at the end where the athletes were threw the green chemical flares they had been given on the way into the Stadium, down to the competitors assembled below them. Several Frisbee games were going on among the athletes, and a few gymnasts entertained the audience with cartwheels and flips.

For some reason, there was a delay of over an hour before things really started to happen. But we didn't care:

many of us had had a few drinks before or indeed carried hip flasks, and the party atmosphere continued. Some of the more daring even took out joints and started toking up. The giant screen showed highlights from the Games, including Nadia winning with several of her tens.

Suddenly, there was a buzz in the crowd, as a team of security guards and Montreal police descended in a flurry of activity on the yellow VIP seats in the center of the rostrum. As they started to search the area, we learned that there had been a bomb threat. But even before they finished looking through the stands, a series of cannon blasts marked the start of the ceremony and the VIPs were escorted in with a huge cheer for Mayor Jean Drapeau. He was flanked by Prime Minister Trudeau and Premier Bourassa. Now the ceremonies could begin. The bomb threat must have been a hoax.

Three hundred Montreal schoolgirls made their way into the middle of the Stadium and formed the five iconic rings. Their long white capes were billowing as they danced to the tune of André Mathieu's Danse Sauvage, and then on a cue, turned the cloaks inside out to paint the rings in the Olympic colours. While they were frolicking in the centre, all of a sudden, a bearded spectator jumped down from the stands, and ran toward the middle circle, stripping off his clothes and flinging them in the air as he did so. He danced and jumped around naked among the schoolgirls with his member flopping in the wind for a good two or three minutes before he was collared by the security guards, long enough to be broadcast across the world by the many television cameras that focused on this unexpected show. Was it for this act of unfettered freedom that the Montreal

Olympics would be remembered across the globe? I asked myself.

The performance of this streaker was followed by what appeared to be a large group of aboriginal Canadians who led the athletes' parade into the Stadium in an arrow-shaped formation. There must have been five hundred or so of them, all dressed in their ceremonial garb. Only later did we find out that only about half of these marchers were really natives, the rest Caucasians: the organizers had difficulty in convincing enough aboriginals to get dressed up in what was presented to the spectators as traditional costume, but to them was just a Hollywood style portrayal to the world of who they were.

Nevertheless, behind these "native" Canadians came the six chosen competitors from each country, led by an athlete who had distinguished him or herself carrying the national flag. For Canada, the flag carrier was Greg Joy, who had won the silver the day before in the high jump. But this parade was already very casual, and as the athletes streamed in, it disintegrated completely. Then all the athletes, including those of us at the far end, the supposed and real aboriginals, schoolgirls and other participants in the closing ceremony started dancing. I saw my sister, Clara, and some of the other Olympic hostesses in their red uniforms join in, abandoning their posts. Trudeau, Bourassa and Drapeau climbed down from the VIP box and shook hands with some of the Olympians. The tie-less dashing Prime Minister even danced with one of the Canadian girl athletes.

The formal portion of the ceremony ended with a procession of the Olympic flag around the track accompanied by a stirring trumpet solo by Montreal-born jazz legend Maynard Ferguson. As this was happening, in this festive mood, my eyes went to the giant scoreboard where bold letters spelled out the farewell words: "Adieu Montréal. Á bientôt Moscou."

Would the Games be so successful, so joyful in Moscow? Paul came to my mind, and the thought that neither he nor anyone else would be wanting to defect at the next Olympics, at least that was for sure.

THE ENTIRE OLYMPIC VILLAGE turned into one big party that night. I remember only bits of it, as I, like most others, was not entirely *compos mentis*, imbibing far too much along the way. I looked for Julie or Carla, but not finding either of them, ended up dancing with a little French-Canadian hostess. She, too, was in heat with end-of-Olympics fever and was quite willing to share everything she had with an Olympic athlete. The rest is a blur.

Chapter 15

The next morning, as I slowly came to, I knew I did not want to get out of bed. But fortunately, through the haze, I remembered my promise to Paul, and even though I felt terrible and tried unsuccessfully to kill my headache with a double dose of Aspirin, I struggled into the shower at quarter to nine. I cursed myself for setting such an early rendezvous with my Romanian-Hungarian friend.

He was there already, at his usual table, very agitated, and visibly grey with stress. Clearly, he had not slept a wink and had just a glass of orange juice in front of him. I passed by the food line without taking anything, indeed, looking the other way for fear of throwing up, and went straight to his table.

"Good morning, Paul. So what's the decision?" We were a fine pair to try to carry out a defection.

"I cannot do it, Géza. It would just be too selfish . . . and risky. My parents . . . I could not face a court-martial . . ."

This was sort of what I had expected, on the way over. The cards had been stacked against it from the start, really, when I thought about it. And even more so now that the

Romanian minders were all over their athletes because of the two members of their team who had supposedly defected

"Fine, Paul. That's okay. But then maybe I will just go back to bed if you don't mind."

"Before we say goodbye, Géza . . . let's go for a walk. Just one more time . . ."

"Sure." I owed that much to my tormented friend. But I would have much rather been back under the sheets.

We walked in silence until we were on the path that led by our grassy knoll.

"Okay, Géza. Tell me what will happen if I stay. I want to know."

"Paul, we have talked about this. I cannot give you any certainties." I was losing my patience. My head was still throbbing. My stomach was churning. I needed to close my eyes. "I can only tell you that I can take you to see the Canadian Immigration people in Ottawa tomorrow. They are, I think, likely to let you stay. But I cannot give you a guarantee."

"And will I be able to go to university?" He was again jumping ahead.

"With hard work, probably. Yes. Again, no guarantees."

Several steps in silence.

"My poor mother. I will never see her again. And my father . . ."

"Yes. It will not be easy for them. But the difficult times will pass. Maybe, in a few years, they can come to visit. Or you will be able to go back. You will just have to be strong. And I will help. So will my family and friends. That is all I can offer, Paul. I am being totally honest with you."

126

"All right . . . all right then, Géza. I will stay. But I want to go right now."

Was this a decision? Or just another swing of the pendulum?

"Fine." It was not fine, because I wanted to be alone in the dark. To nurse my poor head. The alcohol content in my blood was still too high to drive, I knew. But that was a small risk compared to the one my friend was taking. "Very well then, Paul. You pack up and put what you want to take with you outside your door on the landing. And then just walk out through the South Gate, turn left immediately and then right on the first street. Rue Perrier, I think it is. My car is parked a hundred yards . . . metres or so up the right-hand side, a green Ford Cortina. Wait for me there."

"Okay," Paul said ever so quietly. And then after a few moments of silence, with more volume and gusto, "The others, my teammates and the rest of the staff, went off to buy farmers this morning. They saw the new jeans Kulcsár and Fenyvesi were wearing, and they all wanted to take some back home."

"I'm glad they didn't ask me."

"They wanted me to go with them, but I said I was still not feeling well. They will be back by eleven, the coach said. The team needs to have a quick bite before catching the bus for the airport."

"If we go now, we will be almost in Ottawa by then," I said, looking at my watch. "Don't worry!"

I watched Paul as he went back toward the building where the Romanians were lodged. I tried to imagine what he was going through, his feelings, his confused state of being. I felt sorry for him, I knew it couldn't be easy. Also, tremendous admiration. And I was glad that I could help. But deep down, I was afraid that it might not work. That somehow, we would be caught. Or that the Canadian authorities would let us down, and send Paul back.

I WENT BACK TO MY ROOM to finish throwing my things in my bags, which, with all the extra fencing equipment I had picked up, was a real struggle, and decided to go get Paul's stuff first. His fencing bag and probably one other suitcase would be sitting there on the landing for anyone to see. On reflection, maybe that had not been such a good idea after all. A dead giveaway in some respects.

Fortunately, Paul's bags were still outside on the open walkway and there was no one around when I got to the door of my friend's lodgings, so I just picked them up casually, and carried them as fast as I could through the South Gate and to my car.

I saw Paul from a distance, happy that he had found my car. He was standing there looking nervously in my direction, and, as he came toward me to help with the luggage, the relief on his face was tangible.

"Man, I thought you would not come. I thought you had stood me up. Or that the Securitate stopped you."

"I still had to pack my stuff, Paul. And then get all yours. So it wasn't easy . . ," I said as I opened the trunk and we put the bags in.

When I closed the lid and turned around, Paul reached his arms out and embraced me. "Thanks, Géza. I could not do this without you. You are a real friend."

"Well, it's not over yet. And you'll have to wait a little longer now while I go back for my stuff." I reached into my pocket and handed him the keys. "But you can sit in the car. Don't drive away though."

Another fifteen minutes, and I was back; Paul had the window open, and the radio turned to CJIM, Montreal's rock station. He was in an ebullient mood as I climbed into the driver's seat and we pulled away from the curb. It was somewhat appropriate, I thought, that, as we said adieu to Montreal, the song we were blaring out the window, with Paul singing along at the top of his voice, was the Beatles' *You say goodbye and I say hello.*

Driving away from the Olympic site and onto the highway toward Ottawa, I secretly hoped that we would not cross paths with the Romanian heavies returning from their jeans expedition.

Chapter 16

We talked the entire way, and I finally got to know Paul a little better. He spoke fluent French and a few words of English, so at least he had one of Canada's official languages and a bit of the other. I was sure that he would have no trouble learning English.

He told me that in Romania, as part of their 'Romanianization' program the government had closed all the Hungarian universities, and it was very hard for a Romanian with a Hungarian background to get a higher education. His lot would have been to go back to the army, and when eventually discharged, learn some trade that would allow him to eke out a meagre existence. Or go on to become a fencing coach, which some of his mentors had advocated.

When we were talking about Hungarian-Romanian relationships in Romania, he recounted how, even though he had already won the Junior National Championships, he was not taken to the national training camp one year because he had rooted for the Hungarian team in an international epée championship, although several other fencers he had routinely beaten were. Teach the nasty

Hungarian a lesson: how petty the Communist world could be!

We talked about his parents, and it was clear that his mother came from a solid background, as did his father. I tried to assure Paul that they would definitely want the best for their son. Even at the risk of never seeing him again. This brought on some silence, as no doubt, the implications weighed heavily on him.

Finally, we were nearing Ottawa, and my plan was to go straight to the cottage that Mal and I were renting on the Gatineau River. Today—the first Monday in August—was a holiday in Canada, so I did not have to think about work till the following day, and there was no point in staying in the city on such a beautiful day. I aimed to relish the rest of this last little time off before having to go back to my job at the Department of Finance and deal with Paul's request for asylum. Although whenever I thought about that, the adrenaline started to flow.

And, indeed, the sun was shining and it was pleasantly warm, as we finally arrived at the turnoff for the driveway of the cottage. Paul could not believe his eyes. The house was on a promontory, with good river frontage, a large dock, a full cottage and two separate little cabins, of which I was occupying one. Mal was not in the main building where his room was, and it was only when I went out on the screened porch that I saw him out on the river in our canoe with two girls in bikinis. Paul and I went down to the pier and waved at them as Mal slowly paddled to shore.

The girls were both great looking and well tanned. Paul could not keep his eyes off the scantily clad beauties. I introduced my fencer friend and quickly told them what was going on. Mal presented the ladies: Cathy, Mal's current babe, I already knew, but the other girl, Maryann, I had not met before. She, too, was very, very cute.

"Hey Boy"—my Expo '70 friends called me that from Japan days—"I know you won't mind . . . we're having a few people over tonight," Mal said smiling. "To celebrate the return of the Olympian . . . the Olympians . . ." In his fluent French, bowing toward Paul and adding for his benefit, ". . . and to welcome the new Canadian." A good diplomat, he was exercising his skills.

While we changed into shorts and T-shirt—I gave Paul one of each—Cathy and Maryann whipped up a salad for lunch. We ate out on the porch: salad, cheese, charcuterie, baguette, a couple of bottles of wine, fruit. Paul and I wolfed the food down, and the wine helped ease my hangover. This was home now, and it was good to be back.

After lunch, we settled Paul into the unoccupied cabin: this way, he had his own little home in Canada from day one. Mal and I off-loaded some more clothes on him, including an old bathing suit I had at the bottom of one of the drawers. And some jeans—"farmers"—and a sweater for later, when it got cooler.

The newly minted Romanian refugee was all set for cottage life in Canada.

PAUL HAD NO TROUBLE settling into the hedonism of our existence. He was the hit of the party that night, the novelty from the Communist world, the Olympic swordsman who had the courage to defect, to start a new life here among us. He loved the simple Canadian meal of steaks grilled on the barbecue, salad and bread and cheese. Tarte au sucre and vanilla ice cream. And lots of beer and wine. The girls fawned over him and competed for his attention. He was at ease with them, since like all good Canadians trying to make it in Ottawa, they spoke French. By the time we got fully into swing with dancing, the competition was pretty well whittled down to Maryann, who had enchanted him in the first instance on his arrival. It was she whom he followed to join in, the to him new but exciting sport of skinny-dipping, and it was with her that he disappeared afterward into his very own little cabin.

Not bad for a defection. Fully outfitted, with your own home to sleep in, and after eating and drinking to your heart's content, even your very own partner to sleep with the first night!

THE NEXT MORNING, with a mug of coffee in each hand, I knocked on Paul's door at eight. I heard a groggy, "Yes?" from somewhere between crinkling sheets.

"Paul. Get up. We need to get you to Immigration."

Time to get serious. I wanted to call Gavin Stewart at eight-thirty sharp and be at his office shortly after nine if he could receive us.

"GAVIN? HI. IT'S GÉZA."

It didn't take long for me to present the situation. He understood right away; clearly, as we already knew, Paul was not the first or the only, defector at these Olympics.

"Bring him in as soon as you can. I'll be here, and I'll get some other people to join us."

A quick phone call to my office to tell them I would be in only a little later and we were on our way.

PAUL WAS NERVOUS as we took the elevator up to the eighth floor where Gavin's office was. Fortunately, there was no time for him to worry too much though, as we were ushered right into a conference room. Six people were occupying seats in there already, of whom, I only knew Gavin.

Gavin showed Paul to a chair across the table from the bureaucrats, in the centre. One of these was a translator, two were junior colleagues of Gavin, and two were from the intelligence bureau of the RCMP, the Royal Canadian Mounted Police, Canada's answer to the CIA and FBI, combined. I sat down beside Paul, although my role in Paul's defection was, for all intents and purposes, finished.

It was quickly established that Paul spoke French. The meeting, though, ended up being in four languages: French, with Gavin and his two colleagues, translation from Romanian or French to English for the RCMP, and occasionally Hungarian between just Paul and me.

Gavin chaired the meeting.

"So, Mr. Szabó. I understand from Mr. Tatrallyay that you would like to request political asylum in Canada."

"Yes, sir."

"On what grounds?" one of Gavin's colleagues asked.

"The Hungarian minority in Romania is discriminated against . . ." I started to answer. Gavin gave me a look which told me that I should let Paul do the talking.

"We are oppressed by the government." Paul took over. "My family is Hungarian."

"If you go back, would you be put in jail?" Gavin's other colleague asked.

"Yes. Or worse. I am in the army. I would be considered a deserter. They could shoot me."

"What is your rank?" one of the RCMP asked.

"Sergeant Major . . ."

"Hmmm. That's impressive . . ." This from the other RCMP officer as he jotted it down.

"But I never had any active role in the military . . ." Paul tried to downplay the rank.

"Nevertheless, he could still be executed . . ." I chimed in to stress the gravity of the situation.

The two intelligence officers alternated in asking a number of questions about exactly what Paul's role in the army had been, where he had been stationed, who his commanders were and so on. They took notes of all this too. I listened in silence for a while, but eventually, when there was a lull, interjected.

"Pretty well all the Romanian athletes are in the armed forces. All young people have to serve there."

Everyone ignored me and I realized I had voiced the obvious.

"Who do you know in Canada?" one of the RCMP asked changing the subject, "Besides . . . Mr. . . . Tatrallyay."

"Well . . . I met some people last night. And . . . there were some Canadian athletes at the Olympics."

"Do you know anyone else?"

Paul paused a while before he answered. "Yes . . . there is a girl. A woman I knew back in Romania who defected two years ago. In Rome, I believe. She was there with the Romanian basketball team. She came to Canada and is here now."

"Where?"

"I don't really know . . . But I saw her in Montreal. She was also friends with one of the other fencers."

"What is her name?"

"Szabó Kinga. Same family name as mine."

"A relative?"

"No . . . a friend."

"Szabó means 'tailor' in Hungarian," I interjected, trying to be helpful. "It is a common name, just like 'Taylor' here . . ."

"How do you know her?" one of the RCMP officers asked, ignoring my lame comment.

"We met . . . in Moscow . . . at the World University Championships."

"How?" The interrogator was persistent.

"She overheard me talking in Hungarian with a friend from the team. At the airport, as we were leaving. She had quite a chuckle that my last name was also Szabó. She then went ahead and reserved a seat beside me for the flight back to Bucharest. That three and a half hour flight cemented a strong friendship."

"And then?"

"She also lived in Kolozsvár . . . Cluj-Napoca, as they call it in Romanian. I saw her occasionally, but there was school, and fencing . . . and basketball for her."

"Well, Mr. Szabó, could you please write her name down for us," the older RCMP officer asked, ignoring me and handing Paul his pad.

And, as Paul started writing, "Do you know why she came to Canada?"

"She had a friend here. Her boyfriend, I think, had come earlier." I saw Paul fidget a little so this was maybe not a comfortable subject for him.

"Did you know . . . this . . . boyfriend?

"No."

"Mr. Szabó, we will take your request for political asylum under consideration," Gavin seemed to have had enough and wanted to bring the meeting to a close. "That is, we will take it to the Minister for his approval. Until then, we will grant you permission to stay in Canada. We will have a temporary permit for you tomorrow and some forms to sign. Come back at nine."

"Thank you," Paul said, somewhat bewildered, as he got up to shake hands with Gavin and the others.

"Gavin, what are the chances?" I asked as we left the conference room.

"Difficult. No clear rationale for political asylum."

"Surely, you would not send him back!"

"There have been cases. But the Minister could also allow him to stay on humanitarian grounds . . ."

"I thought there were lots of defections at the Olympics."

"Yes, we have received a few requests for asylum. Not as many as we expected. One Russian and three other Romanians. But . . . just so you know . . . both governments are putting lots of pressure on us to return the defectors. It is difficult because this is the Olympics, after all . . . and there are other considerations, too."

"But I thought in München, over a hundred athletes and coaches defected."

"Yes, but that was in Germany. As I said, there are other considerations."

"How do you mean?"

"The Russians are even threatening to pull out of the Canada Cup. And much worse still, the Romanians say they will not go through with the purchase of a CANDU reactor if we don't give their defectors back. It makes it very hard for us to help these poor athletes."

Both these would be serious repercussions, I knew. The Canada Cup, scheduled to take place the next month, was the first ever international competition to bring together the very best hockey players from around the world, not just amateur athletes, as in the Olympics. Hockey was sacrosanct in Canada.

And the prospective big-ticket nuclear reactor sale to Romania had been touted in the press for some time. It would be a huge blow to Canada to lose that, denting the important CANDU program and putting many people out of work.

But to send Paul back at the risk of his life? It all seemed a little too cold for me.

"Hmm. Anyway, Gavin, I really appreciate your help."

DEEP DOWN, I WAS DISAPPOINTED. I had thought it would be a lot simpler for Paul to stay. Surely, Canada would not give him back! The country had a reputation for being receptive to immigrants, and especially Trudeau and his Ministers had proved this to me when they agreed to take the three Czechoslovak girls who were trying to defect at Expo '70.

And wasn't this a more clear-cut case? There, Canada literally would have been whisking third-party nationals out of another country, whereas here, the authorities only had to grant someone the freedom to stay. Moreover, if he were returned, Paul would more than likely be court-martialed and possibly executed for deserting.

Well, maybe it was just Gavin holding back, I told myself; although a good friend, he was also a bureaucrat and probably had to be cautious and not build false hopes.

I did not report to Paul on my disquieting post-meeting conversation with Gavin Stewart. No need to upset him. I gave him a few dollars and told him to look around Ottawa while I went to work. For the first time in a good while. We agreed to meet up for lunch and then again at the end of the day.

THE NEXT MORNING we were back in the Department of Immigration again at nine sharp. The same six people were waiting for us in the conference room.

"Mr. Szabó, we have tracked down the lady you mentioned yesterday," the older RCMP official said. "Ms. Szabó. She is standing by for a phone call. Are you willing to talk to her?"

"Yees . . . yes, of course." Paul was a little taken aback by their success at finding Kinga in less than twenty-four hours. They had met up in Montreal briefly, but then he had lost track of her.

The other RCMP official had already dialled the number on the pad in front of him, and within moments, we could all hear a woman's accented voice on the speaker.

"Szía, Kinga," Paul answered her in Hungarian, visibly happy to hear his friend's voice.

"Pali! Szía," Kinga's delight, too, showed through. "I could not believe my ears when the policeman told me yesterday that you had defected. When will I see you?" All the bureaucrats' eyes turned to me, and I translated in a whisper.

After a short conversation, the RCMP officials were convinced that Paul was bona fide and signalled that he should end the call. Gavin told me afterward in confidence that earlier they had asked Kinga a number of questions, and Paul's story had indeed checked out.

Gavin explained as he handed the temporary papers to Paul, that they had to make sure that he was not a plant, a Communist intelligence officer being introduced into Canada. As a sleeper. Hence the call with Kinga. He went on to say that the asylum process would probably take several months. In the meantime, I would be responsible for Paul. He could work or study while the documents were pending, but not leave the country. If the temporary stay was not converted into a permanent one, though, Paul would have to depart from Canada very quickly. Gavin reiterated again that he would do everything in his power to make this work.

I could see that Paul was elated as we took the elevator down to the ground floor. And he had every right to be: he had temporary papers to stay in Canada, the first step toward permanent residency, and he had reconnected with an old friend from back home. At least, he knew that he was not alone in his new country.

Paul later told me that these meetings, and, in fact, everything that happened to him during those first few weeks, seemed rather dreamlike, unreal, but strangely exciting. He was discovering a totally "new world", all the unknown of a strange, but welcoming new homeland. I know, this is the feeling shared by all immigrants when they alight in their new country, but for him, it was still mingled with fear and anxiety looking back at the risky defection he had embarked on. And it was still not fully over yet.

Chapter 17

It was time to tell my parents about Paul. I was planning to drive to Toronto to see them, and I wanted to take him with me. He should see a bit of his new country. And maybe, my father would have ideas about work for Paul.

As I expected, when I called to tell them we were coming, their first response was surprise. They had chided me for my involvement in the affair of the three Czechoslovak girls at Expo '70. But after they got over the fact that I had successfully helped a Romanian-Hungarian fencer to defect, they were very welcoming. By now, they knew their son well enough.

In fact, by the time we arrived, my father had tentatively arranged a job for Paul at the tobacco farm near Tillsonburg in Southern Ontario where my brother Peter and I had worked for two summers as high school students. The tobacco picking season was just beginning, and the Rapais, a Hungarian farming family, could always use an extra hand. Especially, it seemed, an Olympic one. The work was hard but the farm labourers were housed and fed good hearty Hungarian fare. The job was well paid to boot.

So Paul was making his way very quickly in Canada: the first day, he was outfitted with clothes and had his own bed, cabin and sleeping partner, the second, papers to stay in the country, at least temporarily, and within a week he had a reasonably well-paying job lined up. Not bad.

After an early dinner, I drove back to Ottawa alone on Sunday, while my father took Paul down to the farm to start his job the next day. I felt I had done all I could to help Paul ease into his new life. Now, it was all up to him. He would have to make his way on his own.

DURING THE REST of that summer, I did not see or talk to Paul: it was difficult to get a hold of him since I knew that there was only one telephone in the Rapai farmhouse and I would have had to disturb the farming family. But my parents did talk to Paul occasionally and reported that, as far as they knew, he was doing well.

It was not until the tobacco-picking season was over in the second week of September that Paul went back to Toronto. My parents invited him to stay at their place at least temporarily, so early on, we had a good chance to catch up during one of my periodic visits with my family.

Paul told me that he was very happy with the money he had earned on the Rapai farm; he had been able to save almost all of it. So we discussed his desire to go to university, and we all suggested that he would be better off concentrating on learning English this first year and applying for university admission the following year. Although he was impatient to start his studies—he had his mind set on becoming a psychologist in the end—Paul accepted that this would be the right course of action. My father offered to see if he could get a job for him at his office at least temporarily. In the meantime, he could live with them and learn English at night.

I asked him about Kinga, and he said that they had unfortunately lost touch. The only contact during his stint working on the farm in Tillsonburg was a call from an RCMP officer who had said that his "sister" had been trying to get in touch with him. Although Paul immediately surmised that this must have been Kinga, the intelligence officer was not able to give him her coordinates. Paul expressed frustration and sadness that Kinga seemed to be lost to him.

I DID NOT MEET UP with Paul again until the next time I went to see my parents, sometime in October. There was good news: although Paul's request for political asylum had been turned down by the Canadian government, the Minister of Immigration, Robert Andras, whose ancestors were also Hungarian, had granted him special leave to stay in Canada for humanitarian reasons. It seemed that this was just a technicality, possibly less objectionable for the Romanians than outright political asylum. Anything to try to save that all-important CANDU reactor contract.

BACK IN TORONTO, Paul picked up his epée again to fence at the Harmonie Club, a German-Canadian cultural association where my former trainer Imre Hennyey had been the coach. Some of the Toronto-based members of the Canadian Olympic team, such as Hennyey's daughter, Donna, fenced there, and it was the best place in the city for Paul to continue the sport he loved.

After another four weeks living with my parents, Paul moved out on his own, to a boarding house in Linden Street, owned by Lina Gardini, which had two other residents. I am sure that my parents were quite relieved: while they liked Paul, they were at a stage in life where an extended guest was a bit of an imposition. And, no doubt they were happy to have been able to help Paul start his new life in Canada. With the money he saved from working at the tobacco farm, Paul bought his first car, a Ford Capri.

Later, Paul recounted that it was through the Harmonie Club that he was finally reunited with Kinga in the summer of 1977. The story went like this:

One day Kinga was riding the subway home from work just as she did every day, and she overheard a man and a woman talking in Hungarian about fencing. She perked up, closed the book she was reading, and addressed the couple in her native language, asking whether by any chance they knew Paul Szabó, an Olympic fencer from Transylvania. As it happened, the man was Ernie Meiszter, one of the coaches of our Olympic team, who now taught at the Harmonie Club.

And of course, he knew Paul.

Kinga showed up at the Club the very next day after work, and Paul was delighted to see a familiar face from home. That very evening after fencing, they had dinner together and talked about their common history.

They started seeing each other regularly, and the next time I went home, my mother told Paul to invite Kinga for dinner. She was a tall, slender, good-looking woman, with a personality that matched her physical strength. My mother made a delicious Chicken Paprikás with nokedli (little dumplings), an iconic Hungarian dish, and both Paul and Kinga enjoyed the good home-cooked food and familial atmosphere.

It was right around this time too, that the Canadian government selected me as Technical Assistant to the Executive Director for Canada at the Inter-American Development Bank in Washington D.C. The job was to start in January 1977, so there was not much time to visit and say goodbye. I was very pleased because this would get me out of Ottawa, which was far too cold in the winter and, for my taste, socially a bit on the boring side.

MOVING AWAY FROM CANADA meant that I was less and less in touch with Paul. On my rare visits to Toronto, at first I tried to see Kinga and him, or at the very least talk to them on the phone. But the time I had was always so short, and I wanted to devote as much of it as possible to my parents and sister. My mother had been diagnosed with breast cancer that had metastasized to the lung and my youngest sister had learning disabilities and other health issues, so of course, they were my priorities.

Soon after moving to Washington, I gave up fencing for good. It just seemed to have lost its attractiveness: since I was hardly practicing at all, I no longer had the edge, and in the few competitions I entered half-heartedly, I performed dismally. Better to give up the sport I had excelled in, and pursue other forms of exercise. So, with Marcia, the girl I had fallen in love with very soon after I arrived in Washington and whom I was seeing regularly, we often paired up to play doubles tennis against young couples we had become friends with. Including an old fencing buddy of mine from Canada, Manfred von Nostitz who had been on the 1972 Canadian Olympic epée team and now was one of the senior diplomats at the Canadian Embassy.

Later that year, I heard from my parents that Paul and Kinga got married. In a small civil ceremony. I was happy for them and sent them my best wishes.

Paul started his studies in clinical psychology that fall, at York University in Toronto. And it was Kinga who supported him throughout and put him through school. She had a good job with the Toronto Dominion Bank. I think he still fenced at the University and the Harmonie Club for a while, but I believe his heart was no longer in it either.

In 1980, I joined the Royal Bank of Canada's Latin America Division in Montreal, but later that year they wanted me to move me to Toronto to be part of a newly formed group, the World Trade and Merchant Banking Division, focused on doing business internationally. Recognizing that it was time to settle down, I finally married Marcia and we bought a house together on Wellesley Street. Paul and Kinga came to the reception my parents hosted for us. During these years in Toronto, I saw them occasionally, but we were drifting apart. Our lives were taking different directions. In one of the calls during that time, Paul did tell me that his father had passed away, I think it was in 1981. So he never saw his father again after leaving Romania for the Olympic Games in 1976.

A couple of years later, the bank sent me to work at Orion Royal Bank, their merchant banking subsidiary in London, England, and it became even more difficult to keep up with Toronto friends. I did hear in 1985 that Kinga gave birth to a son, Peter. I was pleased that they gave him the same name as my father. Paul's mother came out to help them with the child, as he was working full time as a clinical psychologist and Kinga worked as a project manager in a bank. By this time, we were back in Montreal, also busy with two children, and I sent the young family a congratulatory note. It made me happy to see that their lives seemed to be unfolding happily and successfully.

Chapter 18

Over the next few years, my work with the Royal Bank of Canada took us from Montreal to New York, then to Frankfurt, Germany. We loved these foreign postings and tried to make the most of them. Especially being asked to live as an expatriate on the Continent, since that allowed us to travel all over Europe. Including, sadly, in 1993 for me to go back to Hungary for my grandmother's funeral. My father, too, came over from Toronto, and in some ways, it was for both of us a marker in our lives: the ties to the old country that remained after this were tenuous at best.

All this came to an end toward the end of 1994 when I was promoted to be Senior Vice President, Risk Policy, and Marcia and I moved back to Toronto with our daughter, Alexandra, who was eleven, and son, Nicholas, aged nine. I was in the prime of my career with the bank, and we settled into life in Toronto again. We bought a house in Lawrence Park, an upscale residential neighbourhood, put the kids in the Toronto French School, where they could continue with the International Baccalaureate program and I commuted by bus and subway to the Royal Bank's gold building at Bay and King.

On the way downtown, my daily routine was that I would pick up a newspaper to read at the corner where I caught the Bayview bus. The year after we came back, on the morning of August twelfth when I took the paper out of the newspaper box, I saw the headline immediately: "Freak Subway Accident Shocks Toronto". This was big news in the city since many people travel on the subway, and the system had a close to perfect safety record. I started speed reading the article. All of I sudden, my eyes fixed on a name: Kinga Szabó. I reread the sentence to let it sink in, and was shocked to learn that my friend, Paul's wife had been one of two people who died in this horrible subway accident.

The bus came, and I got on, in a trance. I stumbled to a seat in the back, and, as soon as I plopped into it, devoured the entire article. The reporter wrote that the day before, in the early evening, a six-car subway train travelling southbound on the University line crashed at nearly fifty kilometres per hour into the back of another train that was stopped at a signal light just north of Dupont Station. The impact was so huge that it accordioned the train cars into a metal seal in the tunnel and killed two people immediately, one of whom happened to be Kinga. Still, another woman died during the night, after her leg had to be amputated at the site to release her from the wreckage. In an iconic Canadian story, all three deaths were of immigrant women. There were also a hundred and forty or so injured in this terrible accident, caused by a combination of mechanical and human error.

I turned to look out the window because I could not control the tears. I thought of Paul, I thought of their son Peter, I thought of poor Kinga. They had fled oppression in Romania and wanted to build a better life in Canada, and now, this? All the happiness, the richness of finally reaping the product of their bravery, their struggle, taken away from them by a freak accident.

And the terrible irony of it all: that it had been a chance meeting of Kinga and Ernie Meiszter on the Toronto subway that had allowed Paul and Kinga to find each other again and build their life together in their new homeland, and then it happened to be a subway accident that took Kinga from Paul.

There is no God!

I DID NOT CALL PAUL until the next day, thinking he would want to be alone with his son. It was a very painful conversation, but he welcomed my expressions of sympathy. I talked about the hurt I felt after my mother's death, and what he must be feeling. He told me that I had meant a lot in their lives. Even though we had not seen each other all that much lately. He went on to describe the upcoming funeral arrangements.

The service was dignified. Paul's mother, a tall, elegant, beautiful woman was there, as were little Peter and many of their friends from work, school and fencing, most of whom I did not know. Marcia and I went with my father and sister, Susan. Mrs. Szabó spent quite a bit of time with us, especially my father. She, too, had lost her spouse. And now her son did too.

Sometime later that year, Marcia and I had Paul, his mother and Peter over once with my family. It was a solemn but enjoyable occasion. Ours is the kind of friendship that one can easily slot back into. Especially when some momentous event happens.

MARCIA, THE CHILDREN and I resumed our expatriate life with the bank later the next year with a move to London again, this time to be Senior Vice President, Risk Management for Europe, Middle East and Africa. This was my second posting to the British capital, and the third time I lived there, and as always, it was an experience that I—we all—really enjoyed. It did not last long, though, as in 1999 the bank chose to pull back from much of its international corporate business and my position in London was being merged into one back in Toronto.

Instead of returning to Canada, however, I left the Royal Bank of Canada and joined a small Hungarian private equity boutique, MAVA Capital, wanting to participate somehow in the creation of a modern, democratic, market-driven economy in the country of my birth. We moved to Budapest and found a house to rent close to where I had spent the first seven years of my life, and put the children into the American School, a high school that again allowed them to continue with their International Baccalaureate diploma studies.

Although for me it was interesting to be back in Hungary, it was a revelation that I did not feel more at home. I had perhaps become too westernized, but in reality, it was the corruption and lack of transparency in the business world and all the petty jealousies that finally got to me. So when our children had both graduated from high school and gone off to university, we moved to next door Vienna from where I could still continue some of my business interests in the region. In Budapest, I had helped start an environmental finance company and I was still a major investor and board member.

In the Austrian Imperial capital, through Marcia's involvement with the American Women's Society, I became friends with Ben Edwards, an American-Brazilian, whom I helped set up a mezzanine fund investing in Central and European firms. A distant Viennese relative, Emmanuel Jansa, and a friend of his, Anna Hofmann, approached me to help get a renewable energy project development company going, and with some Canadian investor friends, we gave them some start-up finance and strategic advice. I continue to be involved with most of these firms, and I am happy to report that they have become successful larger ventures.

We spent close to five happy years in Vienna, returning periodically to see our children who were now both in North America, Alexandra working in New York after getting her B.A. From Harvard, and Nicholas working on a B.A. in environmental studies at McGill University. During this period we bought our place in Vermont, which has since become our family base. On a whim, my wife calls it "the five-year itch" that plagues me, we decided to give up our place in Vienna and put all our furniture in storage. We rented an apartment over the next two winters in Montevideo, Uruguay, and travelled around South America from there.

When I worked at the Inter-American Development Bank at the end of the seventies, I had visited several of the

Latin American countries, but since that time, had nothing to do with them (other than training in Cuba and fencing against the Argentinian team at the Olympics!), so this was a chance to reacquaint myself with that part of the world. We loved these years of carefree travel around a beautiful continent, experiencing different cultures and making new friends.

However, after two years, I found that pursuing my business interests from so far away was difficult, and we needed to reestablish a European base. We chose to live in Bordeaux, France, where Marcia had spent some of her student days and still had good friends. This, too, proved to be a worthwhile experience, filled with interesting travel, friends, good food and wine.

We gave up our apartment in Bordeaux at the end of 2015 when my daughter had her first child, Sebastian, so that we could be closer to them: originally the target was Brooklyn where they were living at the time, but this changed to San Francisco, when Alexandra's husband David was given the opportunity to join a start-up hedge fund there. We have kept our place in Vermont though, which is where I do my best writing.

During all these years of living abroad, although occasionally we did travel to Toronto mainly to see my father and sister, there was never really enough time to seek out my old friend, Paul, although I did wonder at times what had become of him. However, as often happens, chance nodded me to action: my sister, Susan, told me on one of our visits that she had bumped into Paul. His office was next door to her therapist's at the North York hospital where she went for her monthly sessions.

Susan finally gave me Paul's phone number, and when I called, it was like old times. Paul recounted, laughing, how way back when in Montreal, he had waited for what seemed like hours by my car and was so relieved when I finally appeared weighed down by his many bags. And, how, during those first few days at the cottage with Mal and me, he thought he had died and gone to heaven. He told me that after Kinga's death, he had eventually bought a house in Whitby, near Toronto, and moved there with his son and mother. He now had a girlfriend, with whom he enjoyed lots of outdoors activities on the weekends, although they still lived apart, and this gave him a lot of time to read and think.

I wanted to meet up with him the next time we went to Toronto, but he said he would not be there, because he would be driving his son, Peter, now a doctor of immunology, down to New York. Peter had accepted a position there to do cutting-edge postdoctoral research at Columbia.

Kinga would have been so proud of their son, was the first thought that came into my mind as Paul recounted this.

Just before we wrapped up our conversation, Paul said, "You know, Géza. I am so happy I stayed. Canada is such a great country."

Indeed it is.

SINCE THEN, we have seen each other and communicated numerous times, and Paul, who it seems is a bit of loner, a true intellectual, well-read in philosophy and psychology, has nevertheless always been happy to connect. Each time though, I come away with the feeling that he is happy in his skin and with what he is doing and loves his new country.

He did recount that his mother passed away, and in some ways, this was a blessing after a while since she was suffering from dementia.

As for me, I often wonder about the 'what ifs' of history. What would I have become had my parents not escaped with us and chosen to take their young family to Canada? I certainly wouldn't have had the life I did have: all the travel, the great universities, the exposure to so many cultures, languages and ways of thinking, the opportunities I have had in my life, the wonderful woman I fell in love with and the family we were able to create. Yes, I would have had a very different life, but much more constrained and limited, I believe. Perhaps I would have become an academic and found fulfillment in the kind of life my cousin, Mariella, who stayed behind in Hungary managed to have. Or maybe a Hungarian author. Who knows?

Similarly for Paul. What if he had not asked me to help him defect? What if he had been willing to go back to Romania? Or much worse, what if we had not succeeded?

I remember that he had mentioned in one of our meetings that the Romanian fencing authorities had talked to him about eventually taking the position of coach of the national team. A possible path, had he not said back in Montreal, "I want to stay." Which could have meant a reasonably nice life behind the Iron Curtain, but certainly not the one he made for him and his family in Canada.

Or worse, what if he had been sent back by the Canadian authorities, because of the prospective CANDU reactor sale? Would he have been court-martialled and jailed for life, or even executed? Hard to fathom, but fortunately, we will never know.

Certainly, his life would have been a different one, had he gone back. Yes, perhaps he might not have had to experience the sorrow and the pain of never seeing his father again, and of losing his lovely wife in a freak subway accident. But there might have been other sources of sadness. There always are in life. And, on the other hand, of happiness. He probably, though, would not have had the fulfillment of being able to study to become a clinical psychologist, which is what he really wanted to do, of purchasing his own home, of seeing his son grow into a successful and well-educated doctor of immunology. His life, like mine, would have been different under Communism, even though those countries changed later. We would have been much more marked, for better or worse, by the repression, the mismanagement, the corruption, the petty jealousies and all those negative aspects that drove my parents and Paul to want to leave and that lingered in those countries.

Indeed, I prefer the life I have had, and from what Paul has said to me, so does he.

About the Author

Born in Budapest, Géza Tátrallyay escaped with his family from Communist Hungary in 1956 during the Revolution, immigrating to Canada. After attending the University of Toronto Schools and serving as School Captain in his last year, he graduated with a B.A. in Human Ecology from Harvard College in 1972, and, as a Rhodes Scholar from Ontario, obtained a B.A./M.A. in Human Sciences from Oxford University in 1974. He completed his studies with an M.Sc. from the London School of Economics and Politics in 1975. Géza worked as a host in the Ontario Pavilion at Expo '70 in Osaka, Japan, and represented Canada in epée fencing at the Montreal Olympic Games in 1976. His professional experience has included stints in government, international finance and environmental entrepreneurship. Géza is a citizen of Canada and Hungary, and as a green card holder, currently divides his time between Barnard, Vermont and San Francisco. He is married to Marcia, and their daughter, Alexandra lives in San Francisco with husband David, and two sons, Sebastian, and Orlando, while their son, Nicholas, lives in Nairobi with his Hungarian wife, Fanni and daughter Sophia.

A prolific writer, Géza is the author of twelve works of fiction, non-fiction and poetry.